Country Houses
of Scotland

Country Houses of Scotland

John Connachan-Holmes

British Library Cataloguing in Publication Data
A catalogue record for this book is available
from the British Library.
ISBN 1-899863-00-1

Typeset by XL Publishing Services, Nairn
Printed in Great Britain
by Butler & Tanner, Frome, Somerset
for House of Lochar, Isle of Colonsay, Argyll PA61 7YP

Contents

CHAPTER 1

The Power Houses of the Restoration

---

*W*ith the Restoration of the Stuart dynasty to the thrones of
Scotland and England in 1660 the status-quo prior to the military
dictatorship of the Cromwellian Protectorate was re-established.
Although the two nations were united in the person of the Monarch
Scotland was governed from Edinburgh with its own Parliament, Privy
Council and legal system. The enforced union of the Interregnum was
at an end. The country was considered backward and impoverished in
comparison to its wealthier neighbour, and the opportunities for real
power and success were perceived to lie, as they had done since James
VI and I had succeeded Elizabeth I in 1603, outside Scotland.
Opportunities for advancement lay, in particular, with the court,
society and culture established at London.

Contemporary travellers, admittedly conscious of their own superi-

Plate 1
Caerlaverock Castle,
Dumfries & Galloway.
Nithsdale's building at the
centre of the castle with
pedimented and semi-
circular pedimented
windows. (RCAHMS)

7

ority and keen on promoting such perceptions, reflected upon the state of the nation as evidenced in its architecture. They considered it to be both provincial and clumsy, built for defence and not for enjoyment, entertainment or display. Scottish landlords were by and large conservative in outlook and still constructing castles with quasi-Renaissance features. Some properties (such as **Nithsdale's Building** [plate 1] within the courtyard of **Caerlaverock Castle**, Dumfriesshire – 1643) took up the decorative elements of classical architecture without the order and rationale of a completely unified and symmetrical design. The articulation of the embellishments recognised the influence of classical design and motifs from France and Holland, but this was applied in an haphazard and almost medieval manner without a comprehensive understanding of the underlying geometric and mathematical rationale inherent in the classical orders of architecture. Even such simple and basic interpretations as these had long been surpassed by new modish developments and academic research in the more fashionable centres of Europe. The medieval tradition survived, and many contemporary buildings bore only the

> *'contemporary veneer of renaissance ornament to disguise their feudal ancestry'.* [1]

Into this environment the nobility and gentry of the social elite, conscious of their new influence in Restoration society, were eager to show a marked and distinct break with the past. Considerable powers of patronage and political position were exercised by this aristocracy through appointments to offices in the new government at Holyroodhouse. In addition the nobility were anxious to display their authority and wealth throughout the nation. Many members of the aristocracy had suffered under the period of Cromwellian government. Their experiences during the Commonwealth threatened to severely restrict their options at the commencement of the Restoration. Under Cromwell many estates had been sequestrated, titles and lands declared forfeit, and heavy fines imposed for actions undertaken against the Protectorate Government or for actions undertaken in support of the Royalist cause. Such members of the aristocracy found their finances emasculated and necessarily had to wait for more secure and prosperous times, when the levels of their incomes had been restored, before they could even consider remodelling a property – let alone constructing an entirely new mansion.

Others were immediately in a more fortunate position and they set about the remodelling of old houses, or the construction of new ones, to reflect and express their economic and social position, their attitudes, their aspirations and their new circumstances. Such important nobles were James Maitland, second Earl and first Duke of Lauderdale, John Leslie, seventh Earl and first Duke of Rothes, and George Melville, first Earl of Melville. This ruling class wished to be seen as the equals of their Southern and Continental counterparts: equals in taste, sophisti-

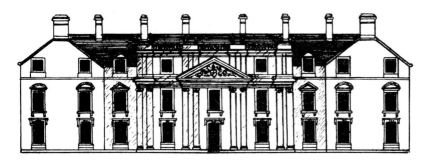

Plate 2
East facade, *Leslie House*,
Fife, 1667.

cation and fashion. Many of them, having also shared the exile of Charles II in France and Holland, witnessed the developing architectural glories of Louis XIV, and some had travelled into the Italian States. These travels were yet another influence on their developing classical tastes.

Leslie House, [plate 2] begun for the Earl of Rothes in 1667, was to be a fitting mansion for the new Lord Chancellor of Scotland. The architect was John Mylne, who drew up plans in June 1667, but died in the December of the same year. The contract to complete the house was passed to his nephew and successor in the office of Master Mason to the Crown Robert Mylne. The house itself was a large quadrangular building, similar in size to the Royal Palace of Holyroodhouse. Its exterior gave greater recognition to classicism than almost any previous building of its type in Scotland, yet it remained within the constraints of the native traditions and craftsmen. The east facade was the most imposing, being a naive imitation of Clarendon House in London.

The plan of the house [figure 1] displayed a Baroque pedigree: designed around a courtyard the ground floor contained offices, servants accommodation, and the kitchens. Located in the east wing were family apartments including a dining room and bed chambers. On the first floor were imposing 'State' rooms – important for the display of wealth and reflecting the social etiquette of contemporary society. The rules of social interaction were taken from the Royal Court at Versailles, the most important Royal Court of the day. To maintain his control over a fractious and divisive nobility, who were often given to intrigue against his authority, Louis XIV created a highly structured Royal Court centred entirely on power and position directly devolved from the person of the monarch. At Versailles rank and influence – and therefore also positions of wealth – were reflected through the access an individual was able to achieve to the person of the King. This was also the only real way of attaining privacy from the company of others

Figure 1
Ground floor plan, *Leslie House*, Fife.
The rooms facing onto the terrace formed a family apartment with views to the south; the servant offices to the north were vaulted.

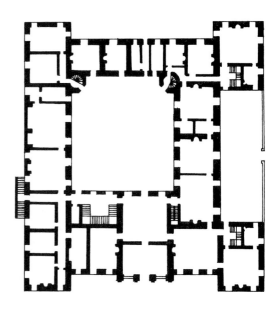

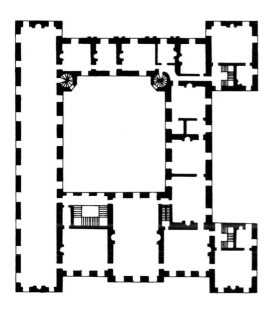

Figure 2
Principal floor, *Leslie House,*
Fife.
The gallery runs the length
of the north facade.

and from the eyes of servants.

The method used was quite simple. Rooms were constructed as a series of interconnecting units, increasing from the most public to the most private of spaces. This was called the Axis of Honour. The sequential plan of rooms reflected the level of formality required within each space. The more public the room the more formal was the social conduct and the entertainments. In addition, the more senior the status of a guest or visitor, then the further they could expect to be placed along the Axis of Honour; with an increasing and commensurate level of privacy and modest comfort that this entailed. This Axis, or **Enfilade**, can be seen clearly from the plans of Leslie House, and also at **Hamilton Palace**.

At Leslie [figure 2] the first floor rooms included a great gallery running 157 feet, the whole length of the house. It was connected to the great stair and adjoined the dining room, the great saloon, drawing room, and the state bedroom. These rooms befitted the home of an important member of the aristocracy, one with extensive influence and pretensions, and, at one time, were expected to house James, Duke of York (the future James VII and II), had he been forced to abandon his claims to the throne before his legitimate accession.

At Leslie House the Earl of Rothes sought guidance on architectural design from varied sources and individuals. Chief amongst these was Sir William Bruce, a close friend of Rothes. In many ways the presence of Bruce and his influence at Leslie House, can be regarded as the starting point for a new understanding of the concept of architecture in Scotland. William Bruce can be thought of as the father of the country house of modern interpretation and perception. Bruce developed an image and a language of the country house along classical, formal, and symmetrical lines. Not yet Palladian in his execution he did use the written works of the Fifteenth Century Italian architect Andreas Palladio as a starting point. His library was known to include a copy of Palladio's *L'Architectura*. In addition William Bruce was to develop the idea of the country house as the primary stage for the aristocracy of Scotland upon which they would display their wealth, vie for attention and express their authority. His architecture developed the country house not in isolation, but treated it as a part of the landscape and as a component of the pleasure gardens set out immediately surrounding the house and those in the estates beyond. This all-encompassing design made the country house owner's social position visible at a glance – architecture was the permanent record of the individual's existence.

That Bruce was able to do any of this at all was largely due to fortunate circumstance, family connections and friendships, as well as a great deal of talent, ambition, and luck. Sir William Bruce exerted an immense influence over the development of architecture in Scotland that was almost out of proportion to the twelve major works designed by his hand. These were in the main country houses, and two of these twelve were built for his own use (**Balcaskie** and **Kinross**). Bruce introduced to Scotland a particular pattern and style of country house plan that his English contemporaries Hugh May and Roger Pratt were also busily introducing to England at the time of the Restoration.

Bruce's ascendancy over other contemporary architects was achieved mainly because of his own aristocratic background. As a gentleman architect he would be widely consulted by members of his own aristocratic class on equal terms. In addition his modestly successful political career on the eve of the Restoration cannot have hindered his progress. (Bruce was in some way partly responsible for persuading General Monck, Cromwell's military governor of the North, to secure the return of the monarchy as a foil to increasing anarchy and disarray after the death of Oliver Cromwell in 1658. He was active in assisting the return of the Stuarts and was permitted to travel between Scotland and Holland with that aim on a pass signed by the General.) Bruce was undoubtedly lucky to have family connections with the highest levels of the Scottish government. His son married the daughter of the Duke of Rothes, his daughter married one of the Hopes of Craighall – both families became patrons of Bruce – and his cousin was the Countess of Dysart, second wife of the Duke of Lauderdale.

As Royal Secretary for Scotland, and a member of Charles II's infamous innermost committee of government the council of the **Cabal**, Lauderdale's influence secured Bruce the appointment as Surveyor-General to the Kings Buildings in Scotland, with a salary of £300 per annum. The post was intended by Charles II to fulfil his personal goal of removing the taints of Cromwell from his realm. The Royal programme was to complete and realise those designs which had been the desire of his father, Charles I, before his execution in 1649. In Scotland this ambition was focused mainly on repairing a few official buildings, and, significantly, upon the remodelling of the Palace of Holyroodhouse. No new royal buildings were envisaged. At Holyrood Palace Bruce worked with Robert Mylne, as at Leslie House, and created a symmetrical facade for the Palace by building a second tower to mirror the original sixteenth-century tower already in existence.

Though Bruce was employed ostensibly at Holyroodhouse by the crown, the majority of correspondence directed to him concerning the building work was forwarded via Lauderdale, who at the same time instructed Bruce on his own building plans for his family properties in Scotland and England – **Thirlestane** and **Lethington** Castles, **Burnstane**, **Hatton**, and **Ham** Houses (the latter in England). Most of this work involved remodelling an existing structure and using this fabric as the basis for formal designs. This work for Lauderdale should be looked at in the context of Bruce's own house at **Balcaskie** [plate 3].

Plate 3
Balcaskie House, Fife. View
of the house showing
Bruce's quadrant links
added to the front of the
mansion and terraces of the
gardens.

Bruce bought the estate of Balcaskie in 1665, and from 1668 to 1674 he set about remodelling it and using it as a place for architectural experiment, interpretation and understanding. He would later adapt the knowledge gained there to the commissions of others. At Balcaskie Bruce enlarged an existing 'L' shaped seventeenth-century house through the addition of a new wing thereby creating a 'U' shaped building. Two two-storied wings were linked to the main house by curved screen walls, which joined the house at two new towers added on the angles of the principle front. At the same time Bruce regularised the building and the garden, and gave the house a formal courtyard entrance. He added extensive terracing and gardens facing the Firth of Forth, and planted the wider estate beyond to allow axial vistas through the countryside and a focal point was achieved by concentrating one of these vistas on the Isle of May, using it as a terminating feature.

More significant than these relatively modest attempts at formal architecture was the construction of **Dunkeld** House, **Moncrieffe** House and **Kinross** House, all conceived about 1676. The only house of this trio to remain today is Kinross House, the second house which Bruce designed for himself. Moncrieffe House [plate 4] was built for Thomas Moncrieffe of that ilk in 1676–1679. The mansion was of a compact tripartite square plan [figure 3] – that is to say the plan of the house was sub-divided by two partition walls creating three main divi-

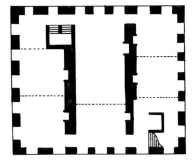 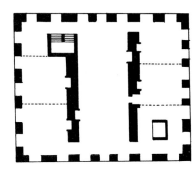

Figure 3
Moncrieffe House, Tayside, 1676.
Left: Simple tripartite plan of ground floor, centre taken up with dining room and hall. The great stairs are on the bottom right with the servant stairs on top left.
Right: Principal floor plan, Moncrieffe House.

sions within the interior. The partition walls contained the chimney flues for the fireplaces of the principle rooms. In elevation Moncrieffe House had four stories: a basement storey for servant rooms; two principle floors contained the main entertaining rooms and rooms of state (for example there was the dining room running the width of the mansion and, directly above this, Bruce also designed a gallery); above this floor was a suppressed attic which contained servants rooms. Dunkeld House was demolished in 1830 and Moncrieffe House was demolished in 1957 after a fire destroyed the greater part of the building. Kinross House is therefore an important survival, and a vital link in the development of not only Bruce's work but also of the history of the country house.

Bruce purchased the estate in 1675 whilst he was still resident at Balcaskie. His choice was clearly made with an eye to the construction of a new mansion and gardens in the most up to date and fashionable taste on a clear site along the shores of Loch Leven. The new country

Plate 4
Moncrieffe House, Tayside, 1676.
Drawn by the author, adapted from a photograph of this house in the collection of the RCAHMS.

house would display at one stroke all the mastery of planning and classical design which he could muster, advertising not only his own aristocratic status but also his undoubted and extensive talents as an architect. It highlighted the knowledge which he had gained from his travels and his trading links with Europe. (After the Restoration Bruce organised the shipment of goods from Holland to Scotland for fitments at his own properties and those of the Dukes Rothes and Lauderdale.)

Bruce's new house echoed the compact plans developed by earlier English architects and the classical designs found in source books of the period (for example Serlio's *Architectura*). His design made best use of the natural level site to create formal parterres in the Franco-Dutch manner to the front and rear of the mansion. These gardens were recognised as amongst the finest and most extensive in the land. Indeed activity from 1679 to 1686 focused solely upon the planting and layout of the gardens and the wider estate beyond. Screens of alder, hawthorn, holly, rowan and willow were planted, fruit trees were established, and broad avenues of trees laid out across the policies. These avenues were

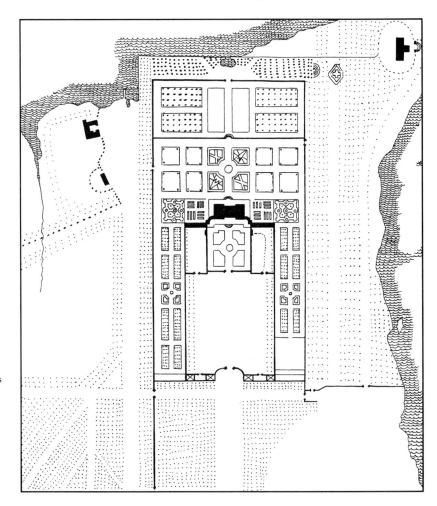

Plate 5
Kinross House, Tayside, 1686.
Garden design showing the formal layout, parterres and planned avenues and trees. Bruce's mansion is at the centre of the design surrounded by formal courtyards and garden pavilions. Top left is the old Kinross House in which Bruce lived whilst his new house was built.

of ash, elm, oak, and Scots pine. They can be clearly seen on Bruce's plans for Kinross [plate 5].

The formality of the garden complemented the formality of the house, the architecture and the society of the day. The symmetrical design was evidence of the order that man was able to impose upon his environment, and stemmed from contemporary philosophies enshrining man as the instrument of his own destiny and the ruler of nature. This was a very labour intensive form of garden design, requiring large numbers of ground and gardens staff to maintain the parterres and planted beds in the best condition. It was therefore another symbol of the wealth of the country house owner – only the very top layer of society could afford to service such expensive estates. It was the expected norm for the aristocracy to display their power with such geometric and grandiose designs. House, garden and estate were all participants in the creation of the image of power – they were devices which reflected the realities of society, ambition, and wealth.

Bruce believed that it was important to establish the formal garden and landscape before any building work would begin on a country house itself. Perhaps this approach to design was adopted because, after his fall from Royal favour and as his political allegiances were suspect, Bruce was placed under virtual house arrest at the estate of Kinross. His activities as an architect were severely restricted. However Bruce managed to continue designing and planning country houses through using trusted assistants. Firstly he would obtain a detailed and very accurate topographical map of the estate and the proposed site of any building. The maps allowed Bruce to visualise the estate for which he was designing without him actually visiting the property. Beginning with the garden design also permitted Bruce to obtain an element of control over the house and its surroundings. Both should, in his opinion, be treated with classical symmetry and regularity. Beginning thus with the gardens allowed Bruce to provide a suitable formal setting to reflect the classicism of his country houses. In addition, by the time that building on the country house was begun the gardens, having been planted earlier, would be at least a little advanced ensuring that the mansion was not standing in isolation.

In correspondence with the Earl of Annandale, covering discussions over the building of **Craigiehall** for the Earl, Bruce was to advocate clearly the formal aesthetic:

> '… where I make any designe I have no regard to irregular planting, office, houses, or any other old matter wch are oblique and not agreeable to a modish and regullar designe'. [2]

Elsewhere Bruce was to write to Annandale in similar terms, when the Earl considered retaining some of the old features of the estate:

> '… and your Lo. will have things proper, modish and convenient you must not concern yourself for anything old in ye way yrof,

Plate 6
Kinross House, Tayside.
Aerial view showing the
garden terraces to Loch
Leven.
(RCAHMS)

especially a little orchard: fruit trees are of no esteem in a countrie where fruit is to be had: its regular gardens, courts and avenues warmbly planted with sturdy barren timber yts in esteem'. [3]

Building work on the basement, or rustic, storey of Kinross House began in 1686, and lasted until 1693 [plate 6]. All the while Sir William lived in the old New House of Loch Leven, just to the west of his new mansion – this was a seventeenth-century tower house which he had bought together with his estate. By 1700 Bruce was to estimate that the total cost of his mansion, inside and out, was some £10,000. This expenditure had put considerable strain on his diminishing resources. Already Bruce had lost the position of Surveyor-General; when Holyroodhouse had been completed Bruce was dismissed from the office. He had also fallen out of favour with the new monarch, James VII and II, who was seemingly overly suspicious of everyone at his court or within his retinue. James VII and II was soon to lose his throne, like his father before him, in a revolution – that of 1688.

In consequence of this loss of position, Sir William Bruce was forced to cut back on his plans to make Kinross House the most imposing mansion of the age. He modified the interiors, and economised on the luxurious fittings which he had planned to install. Kinross remained however a vitally important house for a variety of reasons. Its plan is quite significant in its relative simplicity [figure 4]. It was a double pile house – ie an oblong block being two room widths deep and divided by

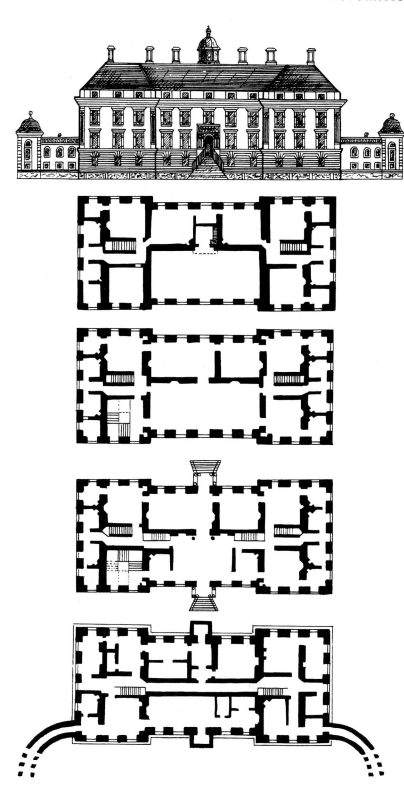

Figure 4
Elevation and floor plans,
Kinross House, Tayside.

Plate 7
West facade, *Hopetoun House*, East Lothian, 1699. The central feature of seven bays is much as Bruce designed it. (RCAHMS)

a central passage or corridor running the length of the house. The rustic contained the servants quarters, and was partially sunken below ground level. The first floor was entered from a flight of steps rising from the garden courtyard to the entrance front of the house. This floor contained the family rooms which would be used most frequently on a daily basis – there was a dining room, and drawing room and a garden room overlooking the garden terraces towards Loch Leven. On the first floor were also a series of private suites of bedroom, dressing room and closet – these were the private rooms of Sir William and Lady Bruce and were contained in each wing of the mansion. As at Leslie House the second storey of the mansion contained the main public rooms for entertaining. Here Bruce designed a double height saloon (with a musicians' gallery accessible from the third floor), a dining and drawing room.

One point worth stressing about the work of Sir William Bruce is that although he followed the convention of the day and made use of the enfilade he did this in quite a unique manner – he did not merely stretch his design out to create one long facade, with endless sequences of rooms leading one into the other. Rather he carefully planned his rooms as almost distinct units with recognisable individual purposes. The central block of Kinross House is one unit on his plan, the wings at each end are another. Each wing contained, on each main floor, two series of private suites facing each other across a connecting corridor. The use of corridors was quite unusual at this time, and would be taken up by architects in the next century eager to provide their clients with new levels of privacy. In a public age, where little was expected to be

Figure 5
Hopetoun House, East Lothian – Evolution of the house.
A: Bruce's house from 1698–1702.
B: Sir William Bruce's design 1706–1710 – it is possible that the unshaded area was not built at the time.
Redrawn by the author from original drawings/figures used in 'The Building of Hopetoun', Architectural History – Vol 27, 1984 (Alistair Rowan).

able to be, or even could be, kept private, Sir William Bruce attained an element of privacy through the simple expediency of a corridor.

This development can be further seen at the greatest building of his career **Hopetoun House** [plate 7], built for the seventeen-year-old Charles Hope (afterwards the first Earl of Hopetoun). Begun in 1699 this house was the culmination of Bruce's career and perhaps the most mature work of his which is left standing today. The building accounts for the house indicate four phases of construction from 1698 through to 1750, and Sir William Bruce was involved for two of these phases [figure 5]. The first phase saw the main block of the house rise with two separate wings slightly advanced beyond a central block. Only this central block survives virtually as Bruce designed it. The wings were eventually united with the main block and additional, new, pavilions were attached to the house by convex quadrant colonnades.

The plan of the house was, again, somewhat unusual for the period, being laid out in the manner of a Greek cross [figure 6]. The centre of the cross was given over to an octagonal staircase, which communicated to all floors of the house. Three of the four corners of the main block contained private suites of

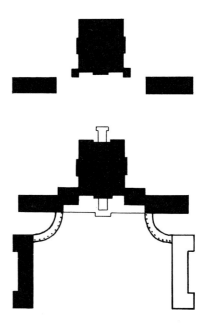

rooms, similar to the apartments designed at Kinross, made up of bedroom, dressing room, and cabinet. The fourth corner was occupied by one single room – the dining room.

The design may well have been influenced by the works of French architects. It should not be forgotten that Bruce was himself in France in 1663 on behalf of Lauderdale, and might well have used that journey to augment his architectural knowledge. Additionally, in 1680 the book *Le Grand Marot* was published depicting designs by Le Duc, Le Mercier, Le Muet, Le Vaux, and Bernini. This offered clear contemporary source material to Bruce from which he could draw inspiration for his designs. Indeed, the original front of Hopetoun House was rusticated in the French manner – the emphasis was placed upon horizontal channelling without vertical interruptions. The whole of Hopetoun was very much in the French manner and recalled Le Vau's **Hotel Tambonneau**.

About the house, imposing formal gardens of flower beds and hedge parterres were designed to enhance the formal continental aesthetic. (During a period of drought recently the traces of these designs became visible from the air [plate 8]). Beyond the gardens the policies stretched out in the formal lines of the *pat d'oie*, the 'duck's foot'; avenues of trees cutting across the estate with views to the Forth.

Figure 6
Principal floor plan,
Hopetoun House, East
Lothian.
Sir William Bruce's design.

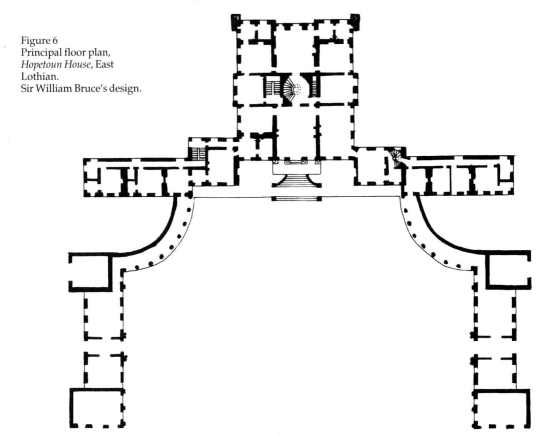

Each of the architects of the next generation was to learn a great deal from Bruce, both directly and indirectly. Bruce, throughout his house arrest and periods of imprisonment, relied on the drawing and map-making skills of others, who might be his eyes, enabling the architect to visualise the site of a country house from his remote position of captivity. This circle of friends and employees would have to act on behalf of the architect, working from his drawings and becoming inspired by his ideas. In this manner Bruce's style, opinions and aesthetic were adopted by those he worked with and by the craftsmen of both this and the succeeding generation. As Surveyor-General Bruce influenced Robert Mylne, Alexander McGill, and also James Smith, the leading figures in the field contemporary with Bruce. William Adam, viewed as the most important architect of the next generation, may even have been under his wing as his pupil.

Plate 8
Hopetoun House, East Lothian.
Aerial view of original formal garden layout.
(RCAHMS)

CHAPTER 2

The Neo-Palladian Movement

―――――――

*W*here and when the Neo-Palladian movement in architecture actually may be said to originate is an academic question. It was given opportunity and prominence in England through the events of the Glorious Revolution which deposed James VII and II. The installation as joint monarchs of William III and Mary II was met with general acclaim in the nation and with bloodshed only in Scotland in 1688. At the time the aristocracy saw these events as really a revolution of, for and by the landed classes themselves to secure their future free from a perceived French influence and increasing Royal despotism. It was a re-affirmation of their rights and privileges to rule the country through Parliament. It was in essence a revolution dominated by the self-interests of the landed gentry. This parochial attitude was encouraged as a justification of their actions by the ruling classes, but it was not shared by William III who used his new position as King of England, Scotland and Ireland to bring the power and wealth of Great Britain to his own defence of his native Holland in its continuing battles against the might of Louis XIV's France. William saw the whole event as a political gamble against his father-in-law, one that for him and his Allies across Europe had paid off. William brought Britain to the world stage as a major league player for the first time in her history, and this was all to suit his own purposes.

Just as the Glorious Revolution was presented and interpreted as an assertion of Britain's inherent uniqueness and distinct national identity, contemporaries at the turn of the eighteenth century called for the establishment of a 'National Style' for the country – one uniquely British. This was made by politicians such as Lord Shaftesbury and the essayist Joseph Addison. The Baroque swagger witnessed in English architecture (witnessed, for example, in the work of Sir John Vanburgh) was criticised and condemned for being foreign. The artificial and imposed formality copied from the French Court was rejected in favour of an easier, less restrictive and more informal style. This was a political and aesthetic challenge to create a style of architecture and landscape design, within the classical pantheon, that reflected the British landscape, society and identity. The source and inspiration of this new movement was to be adapted from the work of Palladio, and the work of Inigo Jones. The origins of the Neo-Palladian movement are complex, and the classical simplicity of the style was admired by many before it would successfully dominate the taste of the nation. The chief propagandists of this style were Lord Burlington and Colen Campbell.

They viewed architecture as a vital reflection of society and the Palladian Movement was promoted through the written word and published drawings as a conscious programme for the reform of British architecture.

Colen Campbell (1676–1729) trained originally as a lawyer in Edinburgh and somehow made the transition to become an architect. In 1715 Campbell produced the first volume of *Vitruvius Britannicus*, a representative collection of drawings and engravings of contemporary British architecture. This work can be seen as a piece of self-promotional advertising for his own architectural practice and abilities, rather than as a coherent statement of architectural faith or principals. But the book nonetheless delivered the message that 'Antique superiority' reigned supreme over the overblown indulgence and free interpretation of classical forms inherent in and developed by architects of the Baroque. Palladio and Inigo Jones were held up for particular admiration. Where Campbell was to learn his craft or obtain his Palladian training is a matter for conjecture. He may have visited Italy in 1697, but this cannot be definitively confirmed. However Campbell appears to have known James Smith (1645–1731)quite well; Campbell described Smith in *Vitruvius Britannicus* as 'the most experienced architect' in Scotland. At any rate Campbell did possess a number of drawings executed by Smith, one of which was a plan of **Dalkeith Palace** and another a variant on the facade of **Somerset House** in London. Campbell's Palladianism appears to have been informed by Smith and Campbell's imagination appears to have been fired by the architectural ideas of his fellow countryman. The English Neo-Palladian movement can be said to have originated at the hands of these two important Scottish architects.

James Smith was originally expected to train for the priesthood, and travelled to and studied in Rome in 1671 for that purpose. In terms of his architectural development – the study of building methods and detailing – the Italian visit would have been vital in influencing the style and tastes which Smith would later have wished to introduce into Scotland. Smith's visit gave him first hand experience and knowledge of Italian, and possibly even Palladian, classical designs.

Smith's plans to enter the church were altered, he turned to architecture as a profession and by 1677 was acting on behalf of Sir William Bruce. His talents as a mason were used at Holyroodhouse. By 1683 he secured the post of Surveyor-General (from which Bruce had been removed in 1678) for himself, though at a reduced salary of £100. His tenure on this position was not affected by either the Revolution or the Act of Union in 1707 – though the salary ceased at this point. It was only in 1719 (some thirty-six years later and after serving five monarchs) that Smith's employment by the Government was terminated with the appointment of Andrews Jelfe as Architect and Clerk of Works for the Highland Forts (a newly established body set up by the Hanovarian administration after the 1715 rebellion in Scotland). James Smith followed in the path of William Bruce, and indeed might even

Plate 9
Drumlanrig Castle,
Dumfries & Galloway.
View to the south-west.
(RCAHMS).

Plate 10 (opposite, above)
Dalkeith Palace, Midlothian,
1702.
The main entrance facade.
(RCAHMS)

Figure 7
Dalkeith Palace, Midlothian,
1702.
Top: Ground floor.
Bottom: Principal floor.

have been more illustrious than his sometime mentor, had he been given the opportunity and commissions to establish his reputation beyond doubt and question. Like Bruce, in so many ways, his activities were not limited solely to architecture. From 1685–86 he represented Forres in the Scottish Parliament, he was a Justice of the Peace in 1704, and stood for election to the Westminster Parliament in 1715 for the City of Edinburgh. After 1710 he was not known to have any architectural commissions of more than passing note.

Smith's earliest work was at **Drumlanrig Castle** [plate 9] for the first Duke of Queensbury, from 1680–90. This courtyard house with its somewhat romantic outlook was perhaps designed completely by Smith, or at the very least built by him from plans supplied by Robert Mylne. At any rate, rooted as it was in the native Scottish Renaissance building traditions it was, as a country house, very different from the works he completed towards the turn of the century, which were in the classical mould established by Sir William Bruce. That is to say they were small, plain classical villas and country houses with hipped roofs and pedimented frontages. It is true that Smith was often working within the confines of existing building traditions which were in many cases limiting, hard to combat and ones which would not easily adapt to the classical and Palladian ideology or formats. He was also, like many architects, being asked to remodel existing properties where major elements of the building could (out of necessity) not be altered, merely adapted. This he did at **Newbattle Abbey** in 1693 and later at **Dalkeith Palace** for the Duchess of Buccleuch 1702–10.

The remodelling of Dalkeith Palace [plate 10] involved the addition of a classical facade and the regularisation of the plan of the house [figure 7]. At Dalkeith Smith, for the central portion of the east front, applied giant pilasters of the Corinthian order which rose the full four

storey height of the mansion. The pilasters supported both the entablature and the pediment for the entrance facade.

The two most important commissions for Smith were **Hamilton Palace** from 1693–1701, and **Melville House** 1697–1700. The remodelling of Hamilton Palace [plate 11] began with the stables and offices in 1682 to designs by Smith. When the designs were to be made for the reconstruction of the mansion proper the third Duke and Duchess of Hamilton sought ideas and drawings from the most capable and prominent architects of the day – they consulted with William Bruce before eventually signing contracts with James Smith and James Smith (his cousin) in March 1693. Even at this point the Duke was concerned to obtain the most modish and fashionable advices for his house that he could afford. In 1693 the Duke took Smith on a voyage south to consult with architects at Hampton Court and view examples of English country house architecture. In addition, the Duke was to obtain the opinion of Sir Christopher Wren upon the building designs provided by Smith. The opinion of leading architects and designers was something which the Duchess would continue to seek after the death of the Duke in 1694.

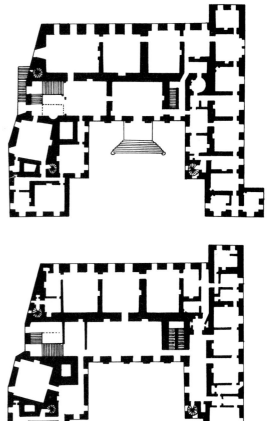

Despite old age and financial difficulty the Duchess persisted after the death of her husband with the rebuilding programme they had inherited together at Hamilton Palace. Where possible the foundations of the existing house were reused – delineating the shape of the new building work. The work had begun with the demolition and the reconstruction of the west wing and the creation of a duplicate east wing [figure 8]. They complimented each other as mirror images. The whole programme was executed as swiftly as possible, with the minimum possible expenditure, and in very troubled times – 1688–1689 being the years of the Glorious Revolution. The Duke was to say of the reconstruction in 1691:

> '... I do not intend to pull down a stone more until we are living in that now in hand and until we see a little more appearance of peaceable times'.[4]

The practicality of such a decision is obvious. However, as it was the rebuilding of Hamilton Palace was to take until 1701.

The basement at Hamilton Palace was neither partially nor fully recessed below ground level: due to the geology of the estate and the retention of the north wing of the mansion. The basement took up the whole ground floor of the house and was given over to the varied service rooms and the offices required to run the ducal lands and the country house itself. The main entrance to the house was from the south, through the 'Horn Hall' (so called because of the extravagant display of hunting trophies arranged about the room), and led, via an imposing, carved oak staircase, to the first floor. Along the north wing was a gallery hung with family portraits; the west wing contained the state apartments of the Great Dining Room, Drawing Room, and State Bedroom; beside this was a private closet with a servant's closet and the servants stairs adjacent.

26

The enfilade ran facing the entrance courtyard side of the rooms, and each enfilade ended in a window which looked out to the south of the estate, carrying the vista out across the formal gardens over towards the 'High Parks' of the Duke's lands.

The designs of Smith follow the general tenet of designs established and drawn by Bruce, but they make less use of the connecting corridors which we have already seen evolving in Bruce's work. Smith's classicism, with its Palladian strength, seems to have been limited to his plans and drawings, to his ideas, rather than being developed in his constructed buildings. It is possible that his designs were too classical for the moment, just a few years out of time. Taste in Scotland was considered to be lagging behind that in England by some fifty years. It would not be until the 1750's when the overt leadership and dominance of Scottish architects over the field of the profession would be firmly and clearly recognised.

Melville House [plate 12] was built for the first Earl of Melville, President of the Privy Council. The house was designed to be

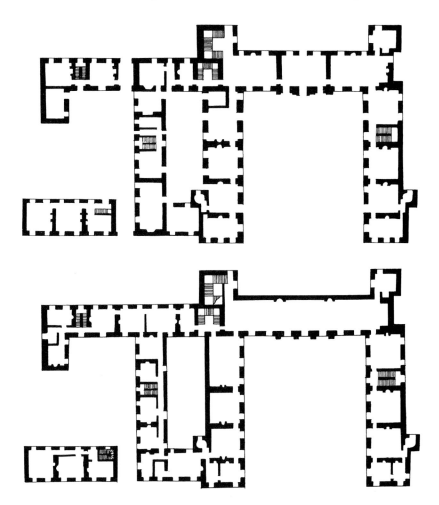

Figure 8
Hamilton Palace,
Strathclyde.
Top: Ground floor plan.
Bottom: Principal floor
plan.

approached from the south, along a formal avenue lined with beech trees. In front of the house was an enclosed formal courtyard, with square ogee roofed garden pavilions. Two office blocks with niched wall screens linked the courtyard to the house. At the centre of the entrance front a series of stone steps rose from ground level to the ground floor. As at Kinross House, on this ground floor and the first floor above were grouped the main public rooms creating a central block. At either end, in the 'wings' of the house, were apartments of drawing room, bedroom, dressing room and closet, with a service stair beside. The enfilade can be clearly seen from the plan of the house, as it can also be witnessed from that of Hamilton Palace [figure 9].

Hamilton Palace was later to be extensively extended by the Dukes of Hamilton to reinforce visually their position as the premier aristocratic family in the land. Immediately after the house was remodelled by James Smith the Dukes of Hamilton called upon the services of William Adam, the Kirkcaldy builder and architect. Adam would continue in this classical tradition established by Smith to become the most prominent architect of his day. Smith on the other hand was probably the source for the next major influence in architectural tastes – the Neo-Palladian movement – and would remain, through the lack of firm documentary evidence in his support, a figure of academic interest and curiosity.

William Adam (1689–1748) stylistically and professionally was the inheritor of the achievements of Sir William Bruce. Adam was:

> '… *the last major Scottish architect whose work was fundamentally different in character from that of contemporary designers on the other side of the Border.*' [5]

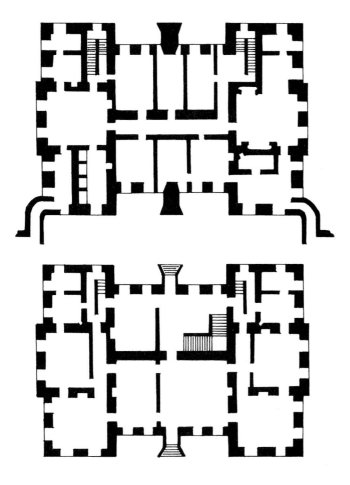

Figure 9
Melville House, Fife.
Top: Entrance front elevation.
Centre: Basement floor plan, containing the majority of servant rooms.
Bottom: Principal floor plan.

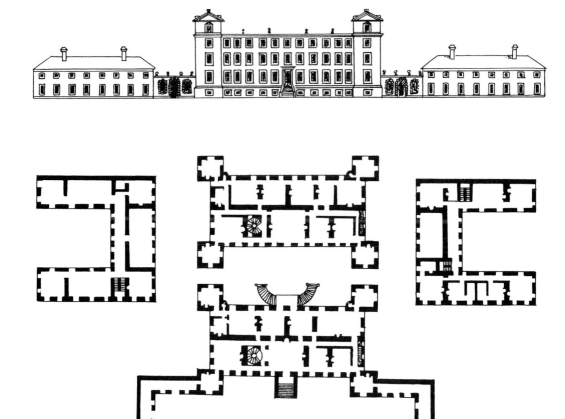

Figure 10
Floors Castle, Borders, 1721.
Elevation and plans of
house as designed by
William Adam.
Top: Elevation.
Centre: Principal floor with
each side first floor of
pavilions.
Bottom: Plan of ground
floor – kitchen and stable
block match each other in
size and articulation.

His early career depended on the patronage and influence of Sir John
Clerk of Penicuik, for whom, and with his assistance, Adam designed
Mavisbank from 1723–27. Adam came from a very different social
background compared to the privileged position enjoyed by Sir
William Bruce or Sir John Clerk. He was a successful builder and
building supplies merchant for many years up to 1720, when he
designed his first building (the somewhat plain and unimaginative
Floors Castle [figure 10] – later to be extensively remodelled by W.H.
Playfair in the nineteenth century). Not a great deal is known about
how Adam established himself as an architect, but this must have led
on naturally from his business interests. Adam must have made extensive use of the library and ideas of Sir John for his formal architectural

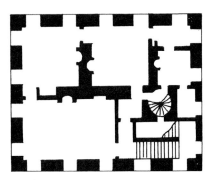

Figure 11
Mavisbank, Lothian, 1723.
Top: Elevation of entrance
facade.
Centre: Principal floor
plan.
Bottom: Ground floor plan.

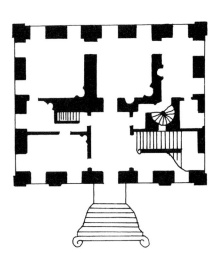

education and for his introduction into classical style and forms. Indeed, the alliance with Sir John was such that as early as 1723 Clerk was attempting to obtain commissions for Adam as his protege.

Mavisbank [figure 11] was intended not as a major country house, but rather as the country retreat of a man of both intellect and taste. It was designed as a small villa, much in the tradition of Palladian experiments. As such it reflected the mood of change and new outlook that swept across the nation. Its source and inspiration were the political events of the Glorious Revolution of 1688 which had lost the Stuarts the throne. It was also a reflection of the success of Sir John within the new Hanovarian regime (and of the failure of the 1715 Rebellion), Clerk being one of the Commissioners for the Union whose job it was to ensure the passage of the Act through the Scottish Parliament – a position for which he could expect financial reward.

Sir John Clerk travelled south in 1727, the year Mavisbank was completed. William Adam accompanied him on this journey. The aim of the trip appears to have been the promotion of a book of 'Scotch Houses' drawn, and for the most part designed, by Adam in the manner of Colen Campbell's successful *Vitruvius Britannicus*. This book was opened to subscribers, but met lukewarm response. Though both Adam and Clerk were confident of the success of such an enterprise their confidence was misplaced – the book was not published until 1810, over sixty years after Adam's death. Campbell's *Vitruvius Britannicus* was to have no rival in Adam's *Vitruvius Scoticus*.

This journey would no doubt, however, have proved instructive to Adam in terms of the houses which he would have visited, the classical style of decoration which he would have viewed, and the ideas on planning and design which he would have absorbed. Sir John Clerk was welcomed by Lord Burlington (the central figure within the English Palladian movement) at Chiswick, and he viewed the other Palladian landmarks in England – such as Wanstead House and Wilton House. Lord Burlington presented Clerk with two Inigo Jones drawings from his private collection. Just as much a propagandist for the Palladian style as Lord Burlington Sir John was no doubt inspired by

Figure 12
Hopetoun House, East Lothian.
Third phase of planned development of Hopetoun House (William Adam).Redrawn by the author from original drawings/figures used in 'The Building of Hopetoun', Architectural History – Vol 27, 1984 (Alistair Rowan).

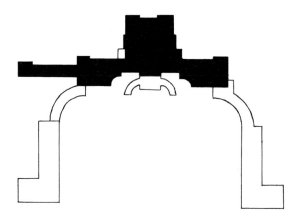

the gift and his visit. By 1727 he was to write a long manuscript poem entitled *The Country Seat* which espoused many of the very same ideas and concepts on architecture prompted by Burlington and Campbell.

> '*A Floor of well proportioned Rooms, to which*
> *By a large open stair or Portico*
> *We may ascend from a neat Spacious Court*
> *Here may a Loby or Salon be plac'd...*'

> '*... Round the Salon may fitly be disposed*
> *Th' apartments for the Master's proper use.*'

> '*... By a well lighted Staircase we ascend*
> *To the chief Floor, with more capacious Rooms*
> *All made to entertain our better Friends*'. [6]

The voyage to London in the company of Sir John Clerk interrupted Adam's work on **Hopetoun House**, [figure 12] which Lord Hopetoun was remodelling barely twenty years after Sir William Bruce had provided him with the (then) most modern classical house in Scotland. Hopetoun was a friend of Clerk, and a keen architectural amateur in his own right. He had subscribed to Campbell's folio, and no doubt considered his house on the strengths of the designs and the evidence from *Vitruvius Britainicus* to be already old fashioned. His choice of the relatively untried and inexperienced William Adam as architect was surprising for such a major and extensive undertaking – and this may reflect the substantial influence which Hopetoun himself had over the eventual final design, as well as the influence of Sir John Clerk in promoting William Adam amongst his own circle of noble friends.

Hopetoun House thus underwent its third phase of building between the years 1723 and 1731 [figure 13]. This grand house was noted by contemporary visitors to Scotland for its unsurpassed elegance and modernity. For example in 1723 John MacKy published this view of the house in his book *Journey Through Scotland*:

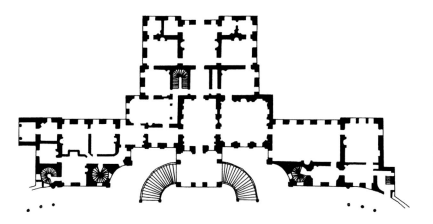

Figure 13
Hopetoun House, East Lothian.
Adam's planned additions and alterations to Hopetoun House.

33

'This palace was built some years ago of fine freestone, exactly after the model of the House of Kinross: but my lord is now adding two semicircular wings of four stories high to the front adorned with pilasters, which when finished will be much the finest seat in Britain. You enter it from a Vestibule, supported with pillars, into a large Hall, floored with marble, from whence runs of each side to the front, a Drawing-room, Dining-room, Bedchamber, and Closet. And behind this Hall, fronting the garden, is a spacious Salloon, with the same site of rooms. The Stair-case is in the middle, between the Hall and the Salloon, and is finely adorned with the history of the heathen gods, done at Antwerp, and put into panels from top to bottom. In the great Dining-room are a great many family pictures, and over the chimney, Noah and his family, offering up sacrafice from their deliverence... The court-yard is collonaded, and adorned with statues and vases.' [7]

Adam's designs for Hopetoun were preserved and recorded in a series of plates intended for inclusion with *Vitruvius Scoticus*. Two stable pavilions were added, largely replacing the existing courtyard structures executed by Sir William Bruce. These stable pavilions were massive single storey blocks, topped by a single cupola tower rising from the centre of the roof. The convex collonades designed by Bruce to provide communication between the stable block and to frame both the house and the entrance courtyard were also replaced. This time William Adam employed a pair of concave collonades, thereby following the more usual precedent found in Palladian designs.

None of Adam's grand schemes for the structural remodelling of Hopetoun's interior were to come to fruition. However as architect, builder and materials supplier Adam virtually replaced much of the existing fabric of the house with new panelling, marble fireplaces, and the like. The extent and development of his ambitious design was limited by the financial expense which could be deemed necessary and appropriate by Lord Hopetoun. However in terms of planning Adam's interior scheme for Hopetoun revealed typical early eighteenth century arrangements for daily life and work.

As we have already noted Sir William Bruce's plan provided a series of apartments around a central staircase. The house itself was designed about the staircase as a central axis. This concept of axial planning was more fundamental to and went beyond the concepts of geometry and symmetry that were promoted by the Neo-Palladian movement. Axial planning was the physical manifestation of the ruling social etiquette of the day, it was the embodiment of the idea of the axis of honour and the enfilade as already mentioned with reference to Bruce's work. At Hopetoun there were additional points worthy of note – architecture which, in fact, made visible the social preoccupations, pretensions, and theories of the eighteenth century. The plan of the house could be divided centrally from courtyard to garden fronts and each half would act as the mirror to the other. To some extent the house could also be

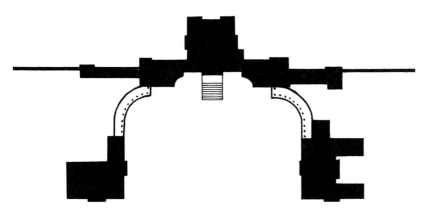

Figure 14
Hopetoun House, East Lothian.
Fourth phase of development of Hopetoun House, reflecting work undertaken from 1735 to 1750. Begun by William Adam, the scheme was completed by his son John (Robert Adam).

divided in a similar manner along an east west axis as well, obtaining a likewise mirror image. This symmetrical and mathematical organisation of space, the cultivation of order and preoccupation with geometric forms was important to classical and Palladian design.

Adam's plans for the rooms in the rustic detailed the servant's quarters [figure 14]. The kitchen was placed in one of the wings of the house, not isolated on its own as was so often the solution in eighteenth century planning, but yet also not really integrated into the house. The kitchen was separated in this manner in an attempt to prevent the cooking smells from passing from the basement into the main house. The kitchen quarters and offices had to be placed just far enough away to achieve this result, and keeping the danger of a serious fire at as far a remove as possible, yet at the same time being suitably close to ensure the provision of edible food for the household. All the varied functions of the house would have to be catered for and within such a labour intensive environment there were of necessity large numbers of servant's rooms included and visible on Adam's plan.

It is worth pointing out and stressing that during the eighteenth century servants were visible. Those servants who worked within the house would spend a great deal of time during their day waiting to be called to perform some function or service. They would be needed to move furniture around from place to place in the public rooms, for example. It was common practice throughout the Century for furniture to be placed right up against the walls of a room, leaving the centre to be spacious and free from clutter or hindrance. If a game of cards were to be played a table and chairs would be brought out to the desired position. When the game was over, or they were no longer required, the furniture would be placed back against the wall, in the positions from which they had been taken. The technology of the country house had not at this time developed to the point of which it would allow the servants to remain out of sight until they were required. The axis of honour, which formed the dominant feature of country house planning during this period, was in part a response to the desire to maintain and develop an element of privacy away from the eyes of servants, whilst at

Plate 13
Haddo House, Grampian.
The Gothic chapel is by
G.E. Street, the renowned
Victorian ecclesiastical
architect.

Figure 15
Haddo House, Grampian,
1732.
Top: Basement floor plan
with (top right & left) first
floor pavilion plans,
servant rooms, stable block
and kitchen quarters.
Centre: First floor plan –
principal floor.
Bottom: Second floor plan.

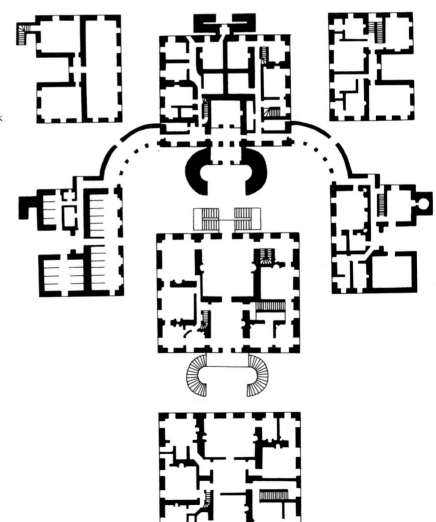

Figure 16 (opposite)
House of Dun, Tayside,
1730.
Top: Elevation.
Centre: Principal floor.
Bottom: Second floor.

the same time keeping them at close hand ready to be called.

The same planning considerations could be seen at **Haddo House**, Adam's next major country house, which he built from 1732 [plate 13]. Here again the figure of Sir John Clerk was important, for he introduced Adam to Lord Aberdeen. Similar in many ways to Adam's previous patrons before him William Gordon, second Earl of Aberdeen was a man interested in architecture and design as a keen amateur. Aberdeen was looking for a designer who could turn his own ideas into reality. His ideas were just as firmly held as those of Lord Hopetoun, and perhaps Adam, who was willing to comply with his patrons' ambitions, was just the man for such an undertaking. At any rate the cooperation of the two men produced a facade which, as originally executed, was elegantly restrained. The pedimented central articulation of the facade created an image that reflected the very essence of the country house. Attached to this central portion was a double curved staircase, leading from the courtyard to the principal floor. This floor was, in the words of Robert Walpole, 'the floor of taste, expense, state and parade'.

The plan of Haddo House [figure 15] is very similar to that of both the **House of Dun** [figure 16] (built between 1730 and 1743 for David Erskine, Lord Dun) and **Duff House**, perhaps the most impressive and greatest of Adam's country houses (built for William Duff, Lord Braco, later first Earl of Fife). Though the plans were similar – almost formulaic in approach – the exteriors were very different.

The House of Dun [plate 14] was constructed to replace the fifteenth century Castle of Dun, and it is considered to be amongst the finest surviving examples of William Adam's work. Lord Dun had employed Alexander McGill to survey the estate in 1723 with a view to building a new mansion. These plans were sent to the Earl of Mar (1675–1732) in France, where the Earl had fled the jurisdiction of the Crown and the

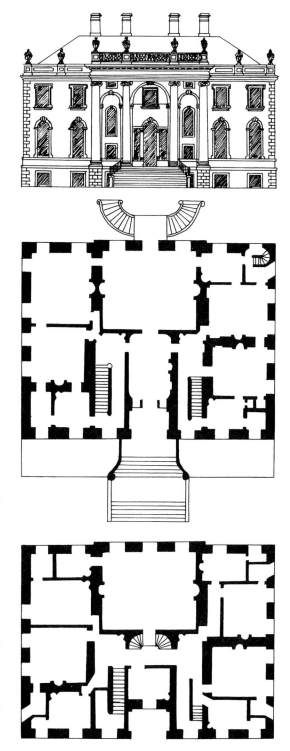

Plate 14
House of Dun, Tayside.
The entrance facade, notice
the triumphal arch motif.

Plate 15
Duff House, Grampian.
The garden facade (with
pediment). Duff House has
an overt Vanburghian tone.

Hanovarian authorities after his part in the 1715 Rebellion. Lord Dun, a Jacobite sympathiser in his own right, retrieved the forfeited estates of the Earl of Mar, and brought them back into family ownership and control. The design of the House of Dun owed much to Lord Dun's Jacobite political sympathies, and the constant stream of advice received from the Earl of Mar exiled in France. Mar, indeed, sent many designs and plans for the House of Dun across to Scotland. These were based on the *Chateau d'Issy*, a mansion built for the Princess de Conti by the architect Pierre Bullet, and a house with which Mar was well acquainted.

Adam's design in turn was based largely upon the sketches and ideas provided by the Earl of Mar. The triumphal arch motif used for the entrance front was not a part of William Adam's original concept – as the planned elevations to be included in *Vitruvius Scoticus* depict a rather flat and quotidian design. In addition the drawings indicate that the house was enlarged in a response to thoughts and suggestions supplied by the exiled Mar. The house was intended as the centre-piece of a large formal landscape garden focused on the Montrose Basin; avenues of trees and formal parterres were to surround the mansion, terracing and ha-ha (sunken fence) were to separate the formal gardens from the wider landscape beyond. Very little of this imaginative and ambitious scheme was carried out, as the estate was already heavily burdened by debts and could not afford such expense. Perhaps discretion may also have played a part in the Erskine family decision not to proceed with the grand plan for the estate – to so readily have advertised the family's hoped for renaissance and reborn position in society might have attracted undue attention, and possible emnity, from the Hanoverian authorities.

One unusual feature of the planning of the House of Dun was Adam's placing of the library. It was normal practice in the eighteenth century to place the library away from the general bustle of the everyday business of the house. Adam, in his designs and plans, would often make a virtue out of necessity, and this rule of thumb was apparent here at the House of Dun. The library was therefore situated directly above the saloon, which

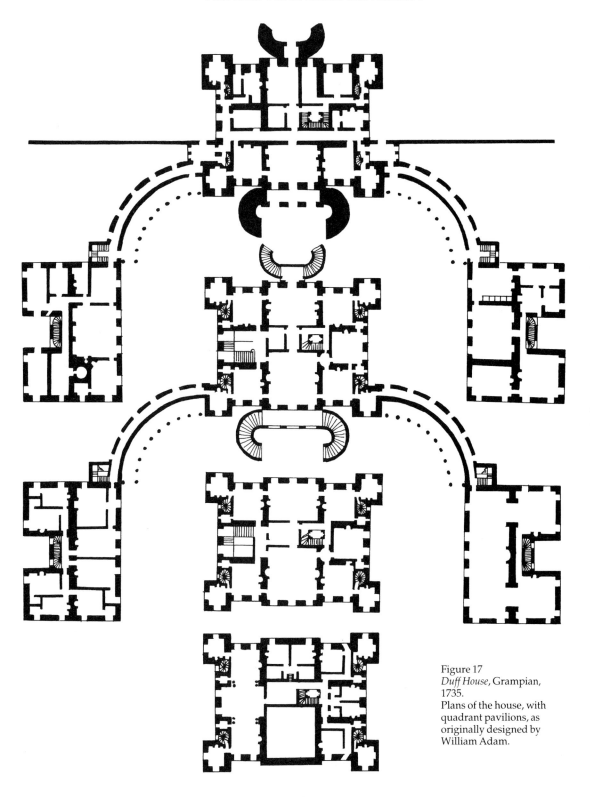

Figure 17
Duff House, Grampian,
1735.
Plans of the house, with
quadrant pavilions, as
originally designed by
William Adam.

– being of double height – would otherwise have created a problem in respect of floor levels for any useful utilisation of this space. Adam included a short staircase rising up from the landing into the library effectively introducing a mezzanine (that is to say a middle level) floor. Crowning all of this, further servants rooms were positioned in the attic storey, above the main rooms and the library.

Duff House [plate 15, figure 17] could be considered the amalgamation of the theories of architecture adopted by William Adam. The main facade of Duff House resembled features of work carried out at Hopetoun House, Mavisbank, Hamilton Palace and Haddo House. The pavilions designed to flank the entrance courtyard in the Palladian fashion were to be executed using the Ionic order. The library (which was almost the same size as the main central block of the house itself) was to be incorporated into the eastern pavilion, away from the main block and thereby also again away from the noise of the house. The mirroring western block was to be occupied by the bulk of the servants quarters. Each of the pavilions was to be a two-storey unit recalling in massing and silhouette those executed at Hopetoun House. Each pavilion was to be topped with central copula, which in turn would echo the copula topped towers on the main block of Duff House. (This also echoes, and is similar in execution to the greatest of Baroque country houses in England – Blenheim Palace – which had been built for the Duke and Duchess of Marlborough by Sir John Vanburgh.)

Of Adam's grandiose plan all that was eventually to be completed was the central block of Duff House. The exuberant design was contrary to the real, somewhat cautious nature of Lord Braco, especially when it is viewed in comparison to the restrained sobriety of his principal seat of **Balvenie House** [plate 16], designed by James Gibbs.

Plate 16
Balvenie House, Grampian, 1724.
Elevation of the main facade, adapted by the author from a plan in *Vitruvius Scotticus.*

In many ways Duff House was too much of an ambitious project for both patron and architect. Both men determined to make Duff House the most fashionable and finest country house in the land and the building as executed displayed some of the highest quality stone carving and sculptured work in Scotland, (the detailing as crisp today as it was in 1738). The massive Corinthian and Composite orders which Adam designed for the pilasters and columns were cut by masons in his works at Queensferry and transported to Banff by sea. The house clearly reflects the great expense and costs involved in the creation of such a premier mansion. Adam himself estimated at the time that the House cost some £9,656.

The issue of the cost of Duff House was to prove difficult and painful for Adam to resolve. The initial enthusiasm with which Lord Braco had undertaken the beginning of such a major project led both men to commence the design of the house and also the building programme without the exchange of contracts or even estimates. Lord Braco may have later realised, when faced with the mounting expenditure, that this ambiguous legal relationship could be exploited to his advantage. He resisted payment for the debts and outstanding accounts presented to him by Adam for costs incurred by him as architect, builder and supplier of materials. In addition Lord Braco was prone to vacillations and abrupt changes of mind over his new mansion, its design, its plan, its style and its construction. The inconsistencies in his approach, coupled with the fact that Adam was again one man providing three functions as the designer, builder, and supplier of building materials for the house served only to muddy the legal and contractual waters even further. Adam had eventually to sue for payment.

The legal case caused Adam great financial upset and it almost ruined his professional reputation. In the event that very reputation was seriously injured by the whole long, drawn-out affair. Potential patrons were cautious of involvement, and had to be reassured that William Adam had only raised legal action against Lord Braco in extremely exceptional and trying circumstances. The prospect of a court case seriously affected William Adam's health, and with some degree of certainty contributed to his death in 1748. Duff House had been begun in 1735, with the main block of the house being roofed by 1739. Adam was forced to issue a petition for payment in court in 1743, but this legal procedure was interrupted by the 1745 Rebellion. When the case was finally settled in 1748, some fifteen years after the building project had commenced, Adam was awarded approximately half of the sums which he claimed were outstanding by Lord Braco. Adam died barely three months after the judgement. Lord Braco, perhaps soured by the whole experience, left Duff virtually as it stood, incomplete and with its interior unfinished for his descendants to consider.

For William Adam it was an inglorious end to a career of great promise and potential.

CHAPTER 3

The Adam Revolution in Style

*T*he remaining years of the eighteenth century can be said to witness the triumph of the age of classicism. Undoubtedly the greatest exponent of the style and the most famous and successful architect of the later eighteenth century was Robert Adam. His architecture spans the close of the era, and shows within the whole range of his designs for houses, public buildings and furniture a calculated response to the contemporary changes in society, taste, manners and academic research which marked the period.

Robert Adam believed that his career and fortune would not be made if he remained in Scotland, and indeed that the country of his birth would only eventually limit his talents and prospects. As the second surviving son of William Adam he joined his eldest brother John in the family offices in 1745 after beginning studies at Edinburgh University. The ill health of his father and the financial affairs of the business would not permit his return to University. Robert's undoubted skills were needed closer to home and when his father died in 1748 Robert was quickly entered into partnership with John to carry on their father's business interests and the completion of existing

Plate 17
Hopetoun House, East Lothian.
The facade and pavilions to Robert Adam's design –
the east front. (RCAHMS)

contracts and outstanding work. Robert's clear aim appears to have been to build up the business sufficiently to allow him the security to complete his interrupted education through an extended Grand Tour. Robert Adam knew that he was needed by his family and by the business, perhaps he also felt that these ties, important though they were, were limiting and he wanted to escape through travel. He was fully aware of his own need to develop as an architect, to learn from his surroundings and to grow within the classical language of the graeco-roman heritage found on the continent. Travel was therefore important. It would at one and the same time introduce him to first hand study of the principal monuments of the ancient world, whilst at the same time allowing him to mingle freely with the most aristocratic of travellers in the kingdom on almost equal terms. Thus Robert Adam could cater to the varied wants and diverse needs of his society and his patrons because he knew precisely and had identified clearly what these desires were, and because he too was himself a reflection of the undercurrent of change drifting through that very same society.

Before Robert left for Europe in 1754 the Edinburgh partnership produced some notable buildings in Scotland. From 1750 to 1760 the brothers completed the final phase of work on Hopetoun House [plate 17]. This remodelling mainly focused on the dismantling of the remaining parts of the entrance front of the house which dated from Sir William Bruce's original plan. For this the principal architect was now John Adam. He established the Second Earl of Hopetoun's confidence in the new firm of John, Robert & James Adam – Architects, enabling the firm to complete work begun by their father. The existing curved stair on the south front of Hopetoun House was replaced with one that

Plate 18
Banff Castle, Grampian, 1750.
The domed garden pavilion is a later addition.

ran parallel to the central unit of the main block, accentuating the facade in a simple yet effective manner. The remainder of the work at Hopetoun was concerned with the reworking of and new designs for the dining room and the entrance hall, for which Robert Adam sent some designs from Rome.

Another remodelling undertaken by the firm in 1750 was that of **Banff Castle** [plate 18], for Lord Deskford. This plain harled mansion was a replacement for the medieval castle which shared the prominent site overlooking the town and the estate of the Earls of Fife at Duff House. The house was a simple and modest piend roofed mansion of three stories, designed with the principal floor on the first storey. The overall feeling was of a small laird's house on a domestic, rather than a grand scale. To the east a two-storey range of offices were joined to the main house by a small walled courtyard.

More significant in terms of its facade and design was **Largo House**, which also dates from 1750. Long an unattributed building, it is now thought to be one of the finest works by John Adam. The house was a single symmetrical and classical block with a pedimented central feature and balustraded roof platform looking out towards the Firth of Forth. In the estuary the Isle of May possibly provided the garden vistas at Largo House with a terminating 'Eye-catcher'; at any rate the main entrance door of the mansion was almost centred on this natural feature. The house was reached by an avenue of trees approaching from the village of Lower Largo, or by a processional avenue leading up from the Kirk in the centre of the village of Upper Largo. The basement of the house contained the kitchen offices, and was unusual in

that the ground level at the front of the house was raised to almost completely obscure this storey, whilst it sloped gradually down to meet floor level at the rear. A small flight of stone steps led from the gravel paths in the gardens to the front of Largo House up to the front door and thence to the entrance hall of the mansion. This particular aspect of raising the ground level to the front of a mansion and employing a gentle slope leading downwards to the rear of a house to subtly obscure the servants quarters in the basement was a feature of country house planning often repeated in many later Adam buildings.

The most spectacular house built by the practice during this period was **Dumfries House** [plate 19]. The house was designed in 1754 and follows the Palladian pattern of planning already familiar for the age. Lord Dumfries consulted Lord Hopetoun for prior approval on the suitability of preliminary designs for this new house. A large central block of two storeys above a rusticated basement was to be linked through corridor quadrants to two pavilions. The ground floor [figure

Plate 19
Dumfries House,
Strathclyde, 1754.
The garden facade. The
pavilions and quadrants
were originally of single
storey. The second storey
and domed towers were
added by Robert Weir
Shultz in the 19th century.
(RCAHMS)

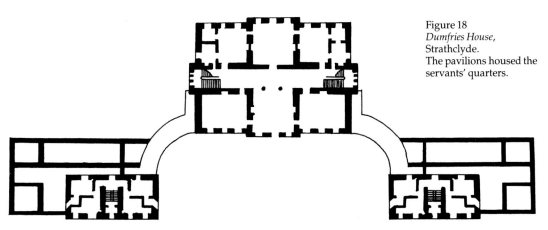

Figure 18
Dumfries House,
Strathclyde.
The pavilions housed the
servants' quarters.

18] contained the servants rooms and the offices of the house. The principal floor was made over to the necessary rooms of state – the Hall, dining room, and drawing room, all connected by a corridor running the length of the house. The plan was both symmetrical and regular. The main entrance facade of the house was nine bays long, with a pediment rising over the central three bays. The servants' bedrooms were contained in the upper storeys of the pavilion blocks. (Their rooms were close to the main house to enable them to conduct their duties, but at the same time they were also a distinct and almost separate part of the functioning of the house.)

Following much the same format the brothers designed **Ballochmyle House** [plate 20] for Allan Whiteford in 1754–57. The plan [figure 19] has elements with much the same emphasis as seen at Dumfries House, though Ballochmyle was a smaller building being built for a man of less ambitious taste and a moderate amount of money to spend. The central block here was only five bays long with pavilions of three bays. The design was unusual in one respect, however, in that the house did not possess a drawing room – merely a parlour which was located (again unusually) down amongst the offices for the house. This recalls the family apartments at Leslie House where in a similar manner country house owner and servant shared part of the same space. The centre of the house was filled with a hall and staircase, with a bedroom and breakfast room on one side, and a dining room on the other. Ballochmyle House was a small villa designed for gracious living. Very little survives today. It was extensively remodelled in the period from 1887–88, and this remodelling deprived it completely of its Adam character and its rather intimate feel.

The first houses to be designed by Robert Adam after his return from

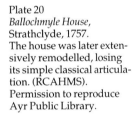

Plate 20
Ballochmyle House,
Strathclyde, 1757.
The house was later extensively remodelled, losing its simple classical articulation. (RCAHMS).
Permission to reproduce Ayr Public Library.

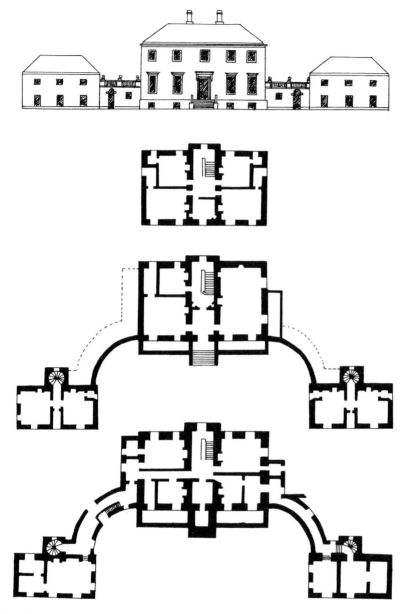

Figure 19
Ballochmyle House,
Strathclyde.
From top:
Elevation as originally
built.
Second floor plan.
Principal floor plan, the
quadrants contain servant
quarters.
Basement plan containing
the servant offices.

the Grand Tour in 1758 were almost exclusively in England. This was after all where potentially the greatest source of commissions and income for the practice could be found. From this time onwards the main office of the firm was to be based in London and was to cater to Southern prosperity. Robert was conscious of the changes he witnessed and which, to some extent, he had anticipated in contemporary life, changes which were happening all around him. He aimed to make and create the very best advantages for himself and his family in the developing society. He had in part learned the lessons which had to some extent eluded his father. He knew the importance in an increasingly

47

literate and style conscious society of publishing both his designs and ideas, and knew also of believing in himself first above all else. This was a period when the published word was the dominant medium of propaganda and self advertisement and promotion. His journey to the continent was not just an education, it had opened up new opportunities and new contacts were cultivated: his travelling companion was the Hon Charles Hope (younger brother of the Earl of Hopetoun); he had persuaded the French architect Clerisseau to join their tour in Paris and under Clerisseau he studied antiquity at close quarters; in addition to all his other studies and, above all of this, he completed drawings and first hand research recording the remains of the Palace of the Emperor Diocletian in Dalmatia. In 1764 Robert published the *Ruins of the Palace of the Emperor Diocletian at Splatro*. The work was the start of Adam's 'manifesto' of architecture. The European tour was to be a touchstone of ideas, sights and memories which were to be the basis of many future designs. It was constantly plundered for nuances of interpretation and Adam used drawings which he had made at source again and again with subtle differences. The repetition of these elements was indeed the key to the success of the Adam Style. It was to be furthered when the brothers published the first volume of their *Works in Architecture of Robert and James Adam* in 1773.

To succeed Robert Adam knew that he had to be one step ahead of the competition, and he knew that he had to provide for a client's particular individual requirements and tastes. Adam was attempting to steal the pace against his rivals in both architectural theory and design. Fashionable taste at the time was developing a growing interest in the literature, philosophy, artifacts and history of the ancient Greek states. This stemmed from Palladian sources and sympathies. Grecian civilisation was also the cradle of modern European culture and society. One striking and important example of this new interest in Grecian style is evidenced by the Society of the Dilettanti, which had organised the subscription of a list of patrons for archeological researches on the Greek mainland (which was still under the control of the vast, sprawling and diverse Ottoman Turk Empire). The research was undertaken by Stuart and Revett, and published in five volumes as *Antiquities of Athens* from 1755 to 1830. Stuart was a Scot, and his contribution to the enterprise was to produce picturesque views of the ancient sites in gouache. Revett was descended from the Suffolk gentry and carried out the detailed measurement of sites. The survey undertaken by Stuart and Revett fuelled the growing interest in the ancient world. It was not just a Palladian interpretation of Roman forms and precedent. The volumes provided clear evidence of the differences between Greek and Roman antique remains and they led others to research not only these same differences but also the antiquities of other lost civilisations such as the Egyptians. All of this research gave architects new insights and new sources of inspiration. In short it placed strains on the stranglehold of the dominant 'official' style of the Neo-Palladians. In particular the *Antiquities* were

> *'designed as both an archeological record and an architectural treatise, a work of reference for scholars and a handbook for amateurs of the Grecian taste... aimed at the patron, not the architect'.* [8]

Robert Adam's approach to architecture in turn pushed against the self-imposed limitations and restrictions adopted by the Neo-Palladian movement. He felt the approach to be restrictive and too bound by rules and the mere following of set down orders and interpretations. Robert stated this clearly:

> *'However necessary these rules may be for to form the taste and correct the licentiousness of the scholar, they often cramp the genius and circumscribe the ideas of the master'.* [9]

In addition Adam believed that the Neo-Palladian approach was uninspiring and repetitive. It was a style which could easily degenerate into a formula that was too easily adopted wholesale by the unimaginative architect. The formula approach resulted in buildings that were designed without inspiration. The facades and the interiors were reduced to basic squares and rectangles without interest. Adam , on the other hand, aimed to create variety both for the exterior and the interior of his architecture through:

> *'the rise and fall, the advance and recess, with other diversity of form, in the different parts of a building, so as to add greatly to the picturesque of the composition... to produce an agreeable and diversified contour'.* [10]

Adam was reacting to his surroundings where laid down rules would be slavishly followed by some of his contemporaries. His architecture would bend and break the rules, his designs proved both successful and financially lucrative. He exploited the distinctly British traits in country house design to his own advantage.

> *'In France where Men and Women live always together and their pleasures are never separate, the Dining room and Drawing room must be both large and are better next one another... But in England, and more so in Scotland, where Men's pleasures in Women consist chiefly as Matters of Fact... it is proper that the Dining room should be a capital good room particularly in the Country and that it should not be next any room where there is or can be company. The Drinking and the conversation after dinner make this absolutely necessary... In the Country there ought to be another room upon the principal which I call a loitering room and it ought to be a library and large. There people spend their time with pleasure who neither like to drink or be with the Ladies. There they may take up one book and then another and read a page of*

each; others may like the children look at a picture book or read the title page and afterwards with importance talk of the book and the goodness of the adition [sic]'. [11]

From the 1730s the salon, long the dominant feature of any house of pretension or taste, was introduced to a rival in the shape of the dining room. Further new rooms were added such as the drawing room and the library as essential requirements to any country house of pretension. Previously the link which had existed between the Salon and the drawing room was one related to and defined by the axis of honour. The drawing room indeed was originally simply a place for all to withdraw to after the function which had been held in the salon was over. Over a relatively short period of time the drawing room became inextricably linked to the feminine side of entertainments and life, when the ladies alone would retire from the dining room to await the gentlemen after the meal had finished. The drawing room evolved and became thought of as a feminine domain and would usually be decorated in a sympathetic manner. In similar fashion the dining room became masculine, often decorated in darker and sombre tones and much more robust and muscular in articulation. It was common practice that the gentlemen would remain in the dining room to smoke, drink, and generally behave in a somewhat unrefined manner, freed as they were from the requirements of polite behaviour in the absence of the ladies. This boisterous behaviour added to its reputation as a masculine arena. Each room and their separate function acted like mirror images of each other. They were often placed in symmetrical alignment right from the planning stage. They acted as a pivitol balance, facing each other across a salon or hall, two opposites with clearly defined territories.

A second major change in the plan of the country house came with the more general introduction of the library to many new mansions. It was originally viewed as primarily a room of retreat, one of study and academic learning. It was, as has already been noticed, often placed out of the way of the daily business of the house. Indeed it was often placed adjunct to or adjacent with the servants quarters. A library was perhaps placed thus within a plan because it was viewed as something awkward, not easily fitting into the usual format of things, and a room which did not in itself have a natural and ready-made, existing mirror within the symmetrical classical designs. But the library nonetheless developed as a room of status and wealth – books though more plentiful than before were still expensive. The library could, just like any other room in the house, act as a room of display – displaying wealth, the ability to collect, and the display of intellectual achievement and knowledge to which the country house owner would lay claim. It soon became fashionable to be seen, or at least thought of, as a man of learning. This path would eventually lead to the library becoming a room for everyday general usage.

Each of these new rooms with their distinct and also overlapping uses were to introduce tensions easing apart the adherence of architect and patron to the tradition of the symmetrical plan. This was particularly true in designs for new country houses. Each new room added a new function and a new focus of attention, entertainment and activity. Each new room was a centre vying for the time and interest of the inhabitants of the country house.

The introduction of new room functions followed on from the introduction of new social occasions, changing values in society, and the development of variation in levels of taste and the variety of fashion. The middle years of the eighteenth century saw the rise and development of 'seasons' of entertainment. For the wealthiest and the most aspiring classes six months would be spent in London (at the centre of court and political activity), followed by one or two months in a provincial city, and only about three months would be spent in a country house. For the few a country house estate, its land and the rents and income generated from the estate, was intended to support a life of luxury. Improved transport facilities (through the introduction of new road systems and sprung carriages) encouraged the wealthier members of society to travel throughout the country. Country houses became reflections of the social whirl:

> 'within the club of polite society, both the grounds and interiors of all country houses of any size were normally open to view, so that during the summer season the more famous and accessible houses would appear like country versions of parades at Bath or Tunbridge Wells'. [12]

Country house life revolved around evening meetings, walks in the pleasure gardens, conversation, tea, cards, balls, masquerades and ridotto (Concert-Balls). Country houses did not lose their position as the important centres of local political power and wealth. A country house was seen as the important, necessary, and imposing centrepiece of a working estate. It was the physical embodiment of success.

The eighteenth century was also the great age for a myriad variety of journals and newspapers which would inform and criticise the select society of the day on matters of taste, fashion and civilisation. This was the age of the Society of the Dilettanti – a select group of the most aristocratic and self indulgent members of the upper classes who founded themselves into a club ostensibly to continue their lives of dissipated living. From their ranks however scholars and academics were to emerge who encouraged architecture, archaeology and all the arts.

To entertain in the height of style by the 1750s and 1760s at least three rooms would be suitable for a Ball – one room for dancing, one for cards, and one for supper. The old axis of honour system used to plan a country house and to regulate social access and contacts disappeared almost completely. A series of interconnecting rooms were used for entertaining, almost as if to reflect the social whirl itself. This form of country house planning was to open up the earlier closed and private

51

Figure 20
Letterfourie House,
Grampian, 1773.
Top: Ground floor plan.
The main room was the
parlour or dining room,
and the pavilions, housing
the service rooms, were
linked to the house by
straight links.
Bottom: The principal
floor. The drawing room is
above the dining room.

Plate 22 (opposite)
Langside House, Glasgow,
1777.
View from the garden, the
quadrant links to the
stables are to the left. Later
additions are on the right.
(RCAHMS)

Plate 21
Letterfourie House,
Grampian, 1773.
View from the garden.
(RCAHMS)

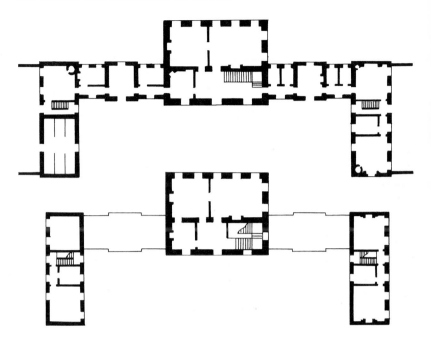

system of state apartments into a more general company, mirroring the circuit of entertainments. Instead of a country house being designed as a sequence of rooms of increasing privacy it came to be designed as two almost separate units – the public rooms, for entertaining, and the private family rooms. The public rooms became a series of richly decorated spaces through which the social whirl should pass with ease.

This idea of a circular movement or a circle of entertainment was echoed in the designs of country house plans. For example Robert Adam's first house in Scotland after his return from the Grand Tour was built in 1772. This house was called **Letterfourie**, and was a small three bay fronted mansion of a restrained and dignified air [plate 21]. Its small size [figure 20] did not merit the introduction of a circulatory plan in full.

Robert Adam's designs at **Langside** [plate 22] of 1777 and **Jerviston House** [plate 23] of 1778 are equally idiosyncratic, but they do provide clear evidence of Adam's response to the new fashions, and also of his own concept of movement in architecture. Adam believed that through variety in external renderings

and treatments, building heights, the orders of architecture employed and variety in the shapes of the rooms themselves, the building itself could be said to possess the qualities of movement. To progress from square room to square room seemed to him to be nothing short of repetitious boredom. He determined that his own designs would advocate the variety of room shapes which would suit their functions within an individual house plan, and that this would logically add to the visual

Plate 23 (below)
Jerviston House,
Strathclyde, 1782.
The porch and second
storey on the far wing were
later additions. (RCAHMS)

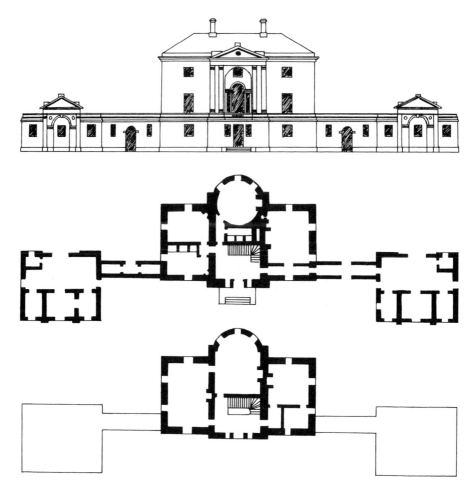

Figure 21
Jerviston House,
Strathclyde.
Top: Entrance elevation.
Centre: Ground floor. The
majority of rooms are
kitchen and servant offices,
apart from the circular
room which served as a
dressing room.
Bottom: Principal floor
with breakfast room,
dining room and drawing
room.

beauty of the house.

At Jerviston [figure 21] the front elevation for this small three bay house was dominated by a Venetian window located on the first floor and also by relieving arch banded by two Tuscan pilasters on each side which effected a triumphal arch motif. The facade was topped by a simple pediment covering only the central bay of the main block. On the plan of the house a circular room in the ground floor was used as a dressing room, the main rooms were on the first floor, and contained a connecting dining room and drawing room.

Langside's plan [figure 22] provided much more interest. The house was unusual in that it was the only classical house built by Adam after 1758 to have quadrant linked pavilions. The rooms on the principal floor show that an oval shaped breakfast room was linked to the drawing room which in turn linked to a dining room that had a bow window projection. The circle was completed by the link to the hall.

Much more extensive in size and detail was Adam's work at **Kirkdale House** in 1789 [plate 24]. This was one of Adam's largest classical houses in Scotland, with a facade stretching to over 170 feet.

54

Writing in 1792 R. Heron stated that:

> '... the house of Kirkdale rises with a
> sort of magic effect. It is newly built, of
> grey granite quarried from the adja-
> cent hills; the edifice stately and
> spacious; after a most elegant plan...
> the granite beautifully polish'd'. [13]

Kirkdale House (pronounced Kirdle) has the
typical features found when studying an
Adam building. The silhouette of the mansion
was divided into three distinct units: firstly
there was the main central unit of the house of
three storeys above the rustic floor; secondly
stepping down in size were the two terminal
wings of the house, which were two storeys
above the rustic; and finally the connecting
links between these two parts which were
only one story above the rustic. By the use of
the step down design, and the varied heights
of the units which made up the design
Adam created a five block building which
naturally concentrated attention upon the
central portion of the house, whilst at the same
time giving it definitive end blocks. Indeed
the effect of varying the height of the units
was to add to the imposing appearance of the
whole.

When viewing the plan of the house [figure

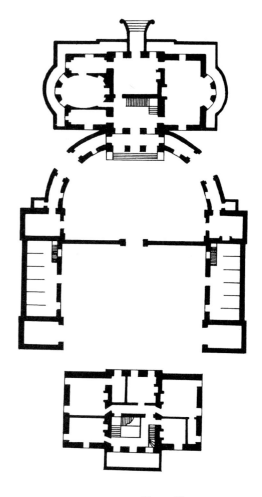

Figure 22
Langside House,
Strathclyde, 1777.
Top: Principal floor plan,
with quadrant lines to
stable court.
Bottom: Second floor plan.

Plate 24
Kirkdale House, Dumfries &
Galloway, 1787.
The entrance facade c.1965.
(RCAHMS)

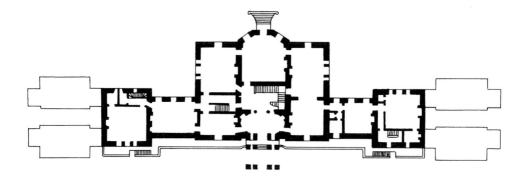

Figure 23
Kirkdale House, Dumfries &
Galloway, 1787.
Principal floor plan.

23] the circle of entertainment, noticed earlier, can be seen to have evolved and was now complete: as rooms lead round one into the other, with each room having equal status with its neighbour. The entrance vestibule at Kirkdale House however was the only room in this particular Adam mansion to be of any really unusual or varied shape.

The largest and last of Robert Adam's classical houses in Scotland was the vast edifice built for the seventh Earl of Wemyss between 1791–1800. This was **Gosford House** [plate 25]. It was completed mainly after Adam's death and this inevitably resulted in numerous changes to his original scheme. The facade of the house was over 360 feet long. The articulation of the entrance front on the east was again based upon the five unit principle, though in this particular case the central block and wings of the house were accented by domes rising above the roof line. A porte-cochere covering the main entrance door was reached via a gently sloping ramp. The ramp therefore partially obscured the rustic in its progress to meet the floor level at entrance door height. The garden facade, to the west, had an echoing and unique

Plate 25
Gosford House, East
Lothian, 1790.
View from the north west,
where Adam had intended
a sweeping semi circular
ramp leading to the
mansion. (RCAHMS)

semi-circular grass ramp. This would have allowed the occupants of Gosford House to step from the saloon straight onto the lawns of the garden.

The plan of the house [figure 24] placed the three main rooms over-looking the garden and each room was to be lit by a single, huge Venetian window. The lighting of these rooms was important as they were designed to contain a celebrated collection of paintings, and, though each room served the distinct functions of dining room, drawing room and saloon, together they formed a grand gallery on an impressive scale. The entrance hall led into the saloon, from which it was possible to enter left or right to the dining room or the drawing room. The saloon was circular with four statue niches, and two matching column screens for the doors through from the hall and those through to the garden. The columns were placed with a typical Adam rhythm and spacing. The central gap was twice the size of the gaps between the column and the wall. This broke all the accepted rules of classical and Palladian design. However, this did make a pleasing rhythm and interesting decorative feature, and was probably inspired by the Venetian window design that Adam had drawn from the Emperor Diocletian's Palace. No doubt the location and site of Gosford House served to remind Adam of earlier days on the Adriatic coast.

At Gosford House Adam met the challenge of the newly introduced rooms, entertainments and fashions through the incorporation of a library and an apartment 'wing' within the main block of the house. Yet Adam remained firmly within the symmetrical and classical traditions of his training in this design, despite the stresses placed by the new social gatherings on country house plans.

Robert Adam developed a style of architecture and interior decoration which gave his name to a period in history, and which would be copied by contemporaries for years to come. He revived what in his perception were the Roman freedoms in the construction of buildings and also the interpretation of classical orders of architecture. In terms of interior decoration this style was as much a calculated business response to the growing archaeological finds at Herculaneum and Pompeii as it was an artistic response reacting against the rules of

Figure 24
Gosford House, East Lothian.
Principal floor plan, the dining room, saloon and drawing room were intended to be one connecting unit.

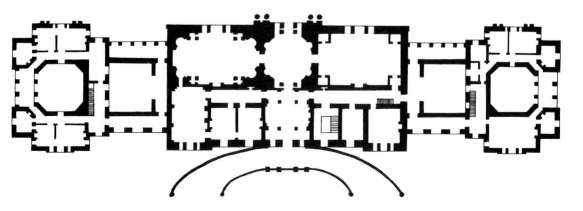

Plate 26
Duddingston House,
Midlothian, 1762.
View of the main house, as
all the service rooms were
placed in the office courts
no basement level was
required. (RCAHMS)

Palladianism, and liberated by his studies on the continent. The 'Adam Style' survived long after the architect died and his family architectural practice had ceased. The style reflected both the needs and the aspirations of a changing society. Adam himself had:

> *'hit upon a brilliant compromise. Astutely anticipating the taste of his chosen public – no longer Palladian and not yet Grecian – he gave them a stylistic synthesis of his own creation'.* [14]

Adam's greatest professional rivals for architectural commissions in England were to be Sir William Chambers and, to a lesser extent, Robert Mylne and Isaac Ware. Chambers and Adam shared the patronage of the King, despite their mutual dislike for each other. Architecturally Chambers had little or no interest in the multi-faceted variety of planning and interior design that so occupied and excited Adam. He was more interested in the adaptation and promotion of the small villa plan, which he had seen in French country houses, to contemporary British usage. Chambers was the son of Scottish parents, but he was born and raised in Sweden. He was a successful merchant before he turned his considerable talents to architecture. His travels took him out of Sweden through France and the Netherlands and on to China. Indeed it was through his studies of Chinese architecture that Chambers came to the attention of the Prince Regent – contributing to the Regency flirtation with the Orient and with Chinoiserie.

In Scotland Chambers designed only one country house of note, and this was in the style of a Greek temple-form villa. This was built in 1762 at **Duddingston** [plate 26], to designs for the eighth Earl of Abercorn. Both the style and the plan [figure 25] were unusual for the period. The house was designed along the villa plan, which Chambers was to use with great success elsewhere; attention was concentrated upon the portico and the hall, almost to the exclusion of all other rooms. The Earl had bought the estate on the outskirts of Edinburgh in 1745 and had firstly set about improvements, through enclosure and sub-division of the estate into farms and parkland, before deciding upon the need for a mansion. Chambers designed a villa for the bachelor Earl, with limited and almost utilitarian accommodation. The most lavish and largest room was the entrance hall, which was sizeable enough so that it would double as a dining room and a public waiting room.

At Duddingston the necessity of large servant offices encouraged Chambers to adopt an almost asymmetrical approach to planning. These offices were placed to the back of the main house, attached to it by a single corridor. The basement was eliminated from the main house, which was itself reserved for the private accommodation of the Earl. In the servants courtyard a stable block faced the servants block in typical symmetrical and mirror-image fashion. The house itself faced a void, having no other part of the building to match it on the opposite side. It was designed by Chambers to appear to be a freestanding two storey symmetrical block. This was achieved by using trees and carefully planted gardens to screen the office court from the main front of and the approaches to the mansion. This encouraged the illusion that

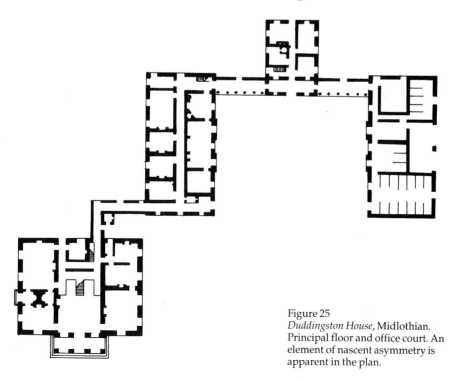

Figure 25
Duddingston House, Midlothian.
Principal floor and office court. An element of nascent asymmetry is apparent in the plan.

Duddingston House was actually a modest temple. This illusion was reinforced through the absence of a basement (with the servant quarters located in a separate courtyard this arrangement was made possible). The windows of the principal floor opened out straight out onto ground level, permitting direct access to the gardens – a link between the antique image of the Greek temple and the arcadian dream of the garden as nature perfected.

Amisfield House [plate 27] was built to the designs of Isaac Ware from 1752 to 1758. It was a conventional three storey Palladian country house. On the main facade Ware designed a triple arched entrance which was located in the rustic. Rising above this basement entrance he created a pedimented logia of Ionic columns. This arrangement gave Amisfield House a strong, central and dominating feature which would attract the attention of the viewer and act as a focusing point and the main decorative feature of the overall design. As with Sir William Chambers, Issac Ware's Neo-Palladianism and Classicism followed a more strictly formal, linear, and conventional approach than the inventive flurries and fantasies incorporated by Robert Adam into his country house designs. In keeping with the contemporary and existing attitudes to planning the main rooms of state, taste and entertainment at Amisfield House were placed in the piano nobile. The rusticated basement floor contained the majority of servants rooms and also was given over to a number of rooms intended for everyday family use. Given the size of Amisfield this arrangement was easily possible.

Robert Mylne was a descendant of the Mylne family who had been Scottish masons to the Royal House of Stuart. In many ways he must have grown up within and surrounded by the traditions of building and architecture. The profession itself must have been in his blood. His

Plate 27
Amisfield House, East Lothian, 1755.
The garden facade at Amisfield House.
(RCAHMS)

practice, despite the very strong Scottish connections, was however predominantly based in England. Like Robert Adam, Mylne was well aware that the major resources and wealthy clients who would require the services of an architect-designer were limited in Scotland. Opportunities, whilst they were plentiful in Scotland, were manifestly greater in England. That said, Robert Mylne did build in Scotland, though few of his houses survive to the present day. One which did was **Pitlour House** [plate 28]. As was so often the case with Mylne's designs this kind of mansion was well proportioned, modest and un-ostentatious. Mylne's style was based on a geometric elegance and restraint borne out through the solid construction of his buildings. He aimed for precision in his architecture, rather than grand overblown designs. The decorative scheme on the exterior of the house was limited to simple geometric shapes and the subtle differences between light and shade playing on the shallow incised stone work of the facade. Mylne's clientele came from all backgrounds, but had a solid base in the newly developing middle classes.

None of these architects (Mylne, Chambers or Ware) can be said to have met Robert Adam on equal terms on their native soil. Adam was immensely popular and very successful, his style readily available and his mind full of invention. Adam was also adaptable, to both the vagaries of fashion and the requirements of his clients. Adam was the consummate architect and salesman.

CHAPTER 4

The Romantic Sensibility –
Grecian & Gothic

The Age of Classicism was perhaps paradoxically also the Age of Romanticism and the two movements should not be seen as mutually exclusive or separate, rather they were shades of the same colour. To be more accurate in the interpretations and the styles of their designs architects had turned to archaeology for inspiration and the search for classical precedent. They also looked to the paintings of Arcadian and mythical scenes by European artists such as Claude and Lorraine for the 'picturesque' siting and landscape setting for their buildings. They aimed to translate the painterly Arcadian dreams into solid reality. Their researches were published as promotional manifestoes of their individual competencies as designers, architects and arbiters of taste. These works in turn became source material to educate and to influence others, from which some would liberally borrow and copy. The many reference works served to encourage those who wished to construct a country house to choose a style of architecture for their mansion which would declare something about their own status, ambitions, or position to the independent observer. Such literature with its continued emphasis on researching the antique and archaeological remains marked the beginnings of architectural revivalism.

Robert Adam appears very much to be rooted within the classical tradition. To a large extent this is true. However he did respond and was sensitive to the changes in taste and attitude going on about him. Not only, for example, was he aware of the stress placed on the symmetrical planning of the country house from new types of rooms and entertainments, but he was also aware of how the planning of the country house was under pressure from new ideas in landscape design. New theories and philosophies of garden design had challenged the rigid formality, and geometry which had dominated the previous century. From around 1770 new attitudes to the countryside introduced and carried over the circular concept of entertaining from the main country house into the garden. Broad sweeps of rolling grassy countryside replaced formal gardens; circuit paths enclosed estates and, whereas before the gardens were divided by a series of avenues acting as axial spokes centring on the house, now meandering paths evocative of woodland walks were deliberately constructed to have an accidental and 'natural' appearance.

In addition to this, people began to appreciate the idea of being able to walk straight from the comfort of their own homes into their gardens without the necessity of descending a flight of stairs leading from the floor of taste (as we have already seen at Largo House). The principal floor was gradually to move from the first floor to descend to meet with ground level. This concept was not new – for example the family rooms at **Leslie House** were located in the rustic with direct access to a garden terrace. However, now in the later part of the eighteenth century if the principal rooms were to move to the rustic the space formerly occupied by the servants offices had to be vacated. A new home would be required for the array of servant rooms. New solutions to their location would require to be found if the country house owner wished to move the piano nobile to the entrance level.

In tandem with these changes came the rise of further new popular theories of art and aesthetics. These were the theories of the 'picturesque' and the 'sublime'. In very simplistic terms the essence of the picturesque was to create a 'natural' appearing environment and landscape based upon the image of painterly precedent. Trees and shrubs were planted to give a garden a naturalistic appearance rather than a formal one. Plants were chosen with a view to their picturesque qualities, that is to say their carefully controlled naturalness and the cultivated irregularity which would add to the effect of the garden. The picturesque was conceived with the appearance of nature, the sublime, on the other hand, was nature in the raw, nature without the control of human influence.

The sublime was based on the concept of the 'little terror' – this was really a consideration of how nature, in all her majesty, and force, could impress upon the individual her powers of creation and also of destruction. Central to the feeling of fear at nature's strength and power was the feeling of safety. A natural feature would be viewed from a position of relative safety, whilst at the same time the dread and awe of nature's majesty could be felt. The sublime fed upon the emotional response of the individual, and the effect of the experience could only be recounted in romantic and emotional terms.

This can be illustrated from the work of Goethe, who described his visit to the Grecian ruined temples on Sicily in suitably 'romantic' terms:

> 'I found myself in a world which was completely strange to me... these crowded masses of stumpy conical columns appear offensive and even terrifying. (I) remembered the history of art, thought of the age with which this architecture was in harmony, called up images in my mind of the austere style of sculpture – and in less than an hour found myself reconciled to them and even thanking my guardian angel for having allowed me to see these well preserved remains with my own eyes... It is only by walking through them and around them that we can attune one's life to theirs and experience the emotional effects which the architect intended'. [15]

Goethe was describing a simple Grecian Doric temple. The construction was crude, but on a massive scale. Goethe's response was firstly on an emotional level, at which stage he recognised all the salient features of the sublime – the antiquity of the remains, their vast size, their simplicity and naturalness, their very crudity, naiveté, and roughness. Elsewhere Goethe was to remark on the 'Barbaric' German Gothic architecture of Strasbourg Cathedral:

> '... Foolishly as a people, which calls all the foreign world barbaric, I named Gothick all that did not fit into my system, from the neatly-turned, gay coloured cherub-dolls and painting our bourgeois nobility adorn their houses with, to the solemn remnants of older German Architecture, whose few fantastical frettings made me join in the universal song: "Quite squashed with ornament". And so, as I walked towards the Minster, I shuddered in prospect of some malformed curly-bristled ogre.
>
> 'With what unlooked for emotions did the sight surprise me, when I stepped before it! A sensation of wholeness, greatness, filled my soul; which, composed of a thousand harmonising details, I could savour and enjoy, yet by no means understand or explain. So it is, men say, with the bliss of Heaven. How often have I come back to enjoy this sacredly profane bliss, to enjoy the gigantic spirit of our elder brethren in their works'. [16]

The architectural response to these extremely varied but interconnected cross currents was manifold. Firstly, there was the response of architects such as Robert Adam. He opted to follow his own interpretation of classical antiquity based on Graeco-Roman precedents, to follow his own artistic imagination, and to cater to the needs, wants and requirements of his clients. In addition, he also sought to respond to the nascent romantic historicism developing in the country and across Europe through a whole series of castle designs. Secondly, some architects opted for whole-hearted revival of Grecian taste and the design of country houses in the Grecian manner. Thirdly, of course, others were to reject either of these avenues and chose to develop a separate architectural language based on the native, indigenous heritage and examples of ancient buildings surviving about them. The close of the eighteenth century and the beginning of the nineteenth century saw an evolving battle of the styles between conflicting periods, methods of construction, philosophies, sources, and ultimately conflicting views of life and society which would never reoccur, or generate such heated argument and debate, to such an extent again.

Grecian taste was part and parcel of the Neo-Classical movement as a whole. It took almost fifty years to become an established style in its own right, and reflected the search by some architects and theoreticians attempting to create a 'modern national style' free of any geographical or historical associations. The apparent paradox that both movement and style were essentially rooted in both these factors did not give rise

Plate 29
Broomhall, Fife, 1796.
The bow projection on the
garden front. (RCAHMS)

to concern amongst its adherents.

In Scotland Grecian taste was, once established, the dominant architectural movement for almost fifty years from 1790 to 1840. Edinburgh was known as the 'Athens of the North' because of her academic traditions and because the city embraced the style. Her terraces and suburban villas were decorated with the Greek orders, and the National Monument to the dead of the Napoleonic wars, on Calton Hill, was executed as a copy of the Parthenon. In Glasgow the architect Alexander 'Greek' Thomson provided that city with some of its finest churches, public buildings and private dwellings all in the Grecian style. Country houses were, however, surprisingly thinner on the ground. The Grecian style achieved an urban dominance in Scotland unsurpassed in any other part of the country or in any other field of architecture.

Broomhall [plate 29] was begun in 1796 by Thomas Harrison (1744–1829) for the Earl of Elgin. Harrison was born in Yorkshire, the son of a joiner. In 1769 he travelled to the continent to study architecture in Rome. He was admitted to the Academy of St Luke in 1773, only after the personal intervention of Pope Clement XIV. By 1776 Harrison had returned to England, where he was to become one of the foremost civic architects of the day, building mainly in a Grecian manner. It was this style that he adopted for Broomhall. The house was originally intended to display the important collection of antiquities acquired by Lord Elgin – these included the famous Elgin marbles from the Parthenon frieze which had been bought by the Earl from the Ottoman

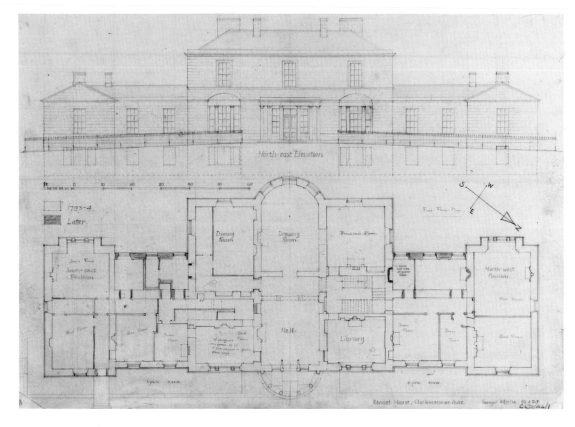

Plate 30
Kennet House, Central,
1795.
Entrance facade and plan
of principal floor.
(RCAHMS)

authorities in Athens. The marbles were sold to the Earl and cut from the temple to be transported to Britain.

Broomhall was not finished to Harrison's designs, and the Elgin Marbles were rapidly sold at a loss by the Earl to extricate himself from both financial difficulties and society's indignation at what some contemporaries felt had been an act of architectural vandalism. Between 1800 and 1828 the Seventh Earl of Elgin commissioned designs from twelve different architects to complete the house. Both the money and the enthusiasm necessary to complete the grand mansion had gone however, and the house was not as spectacular nor as determinedly Greek as had been the Earl's original intention.

Thomas Harrison was perhaps chosen as architect by the Earl of Elgin because the work of the Yorkshire architect may have been familiar. In 1795 Harrison had designed **Kennet House** [plate 30] for Bruce of Kennet, a relation of the Earl's from Clackmannanshire. This family connection would no doubt have been of assistance in helping Harrison to secure the commission from the Earl of Elgin. The ground at the entrance front of Kennet House was level with the top of the basement floor, and gradually sloped down to basement level towards the rear of the house. The entrance front, in addition, had a semi-circular porch, echoed in the segmental-headed windows either side of the porch and also in the semi-circular projection at the rear of the

66

Plate 31
Balbirnie House, Fife. 1815.

house. This latter feature rose from basement to the first floor. The elevation of the house recalls the work of Adam at Jerviston House.

Balbirnie House [plate 31], of 1815–19 was designed by the architect Robert Crichton in a Grecian style for his client, General Robert Balfour. This phase of building was in fact the remodelling of an earlier house built in the seventeenth century and already a mansion once

Plate 32
Blythswood House,
Glasgow, 1821.
Front elevation.
(Permission to reproduce –
C. Methuen-Campbell.)

remodelled in 1777. Richard Crichton extended the existing eighteenth century seven bay house through the addition of a further four bays. The main entrance front was altered from the west facade with the formation of a new pedimented portico on the south front. The whole design was then encased in the Ionic order on a giant scale.

Blythswood House [plate 32] by James Gillespie Graham (1776–1855), built in 1821 for Major Archibald Campbell, and **Stracathro House** [plate 33] by Archibald Simpson (1770–1847), for Alexander Cruicshanks in 1828, are two further Grecian houses amongst the first rank of neo-classical architecture. Both houses were treated in an imposing and massive Corinthian order.

Perhaps more original in design and outward appearance were **Cairness House** [plate 34] and **Roseneath Castle** [plate 35]. Cairness was designed by James Playfair for Charles Gordon, who, having made a fortune from a sugar plantation in Jamaica, had returned to Scotland to purchase an estate in Aberdeenshire. The mansion was built from 1791–97 and constructed out of local grey granite. The half excavated basement at Cairness House was given a rusticated dressing and the two end pavilions on the southern entrance facade were rusticated all over; their tripartite windows mirrored the design of the main door to the house. The two pavilions were single bays projecting slightly from the five bay length of the main block. To the rear of the mansion was positioned a semi-circle of servants offices which was highlighted by striking Egyptian motifs. Playfair's design was not completed in its classical entirety or to the original intention of his designs – both architect and client died shortly after one another in 1794 – before Cairness House was completed.

Roseneath Castle, built between 1803–6 for the fifth Duke of Argyll, was a replacement for an earlier mansion of the same name which had

Plate 33
Stracathro House, Tayside, 1828.

Plate 34
Cairness House, Grampian,
1791.
(RCAHMS)

Plate 35
Roseneath Castle,
Strathclyde, 1803.
The entrance facade.
(RCAHMS)

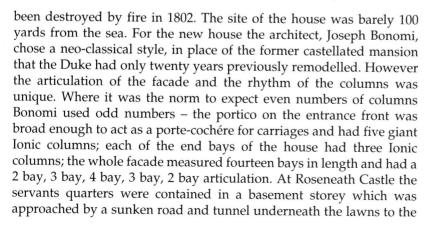

been destroyed by fire in 1802. The site of the house was barely 100 yards from the sea. For the new house the architect, Joseph Bonomi, chose a neo-classical style, in place of the former castellated mansion that the Duke had only twenty years previously remodelled. However the articulation of the facade and the rhythm of the columns was unique. Where it was the norm to expect even numbers of columns Bonomi used odd numbers – the portico on the entrance front was broad enough to act as a porte-cochére for carriages and had five giant Ionic columns; each of the end bays of the house had three Ionic columns; the whole facade measured fourteen bays in length and had a 2 bay, 3 bay, 4 bay, 3 bay, 2 bay articulation. At Roseneath Castle the servants quarters were contained in a basement storey which was approached by a sunken road and tunnel underneath the lawns to the rear of the mansion. In this manner the servants activities were completely hidden from the house. This particular method of planning the servants quarters was exceptional, and not repeated in any other house of note.

Camperdown House [plate 36] was built by the architect William Burn from 1819 to 1823 for Viscount Duncan. The house can be seen as being at an important juncture, a transitional point between the neo-classical style and the contemporary alternative tradition of the castellated and Gothic styles. The plan of Camperdown [figure 26] reflected the numerous changes and undercurrents which existed in society at the beginning of the nineteenth century. It was also in many ways emblematic of the somewhat formulaic planning which William Burn was to re-use again and again for many differing clients across the country. The plan consisted of three logical and distinct areas which joined together to form one unified building. Firstly there was a series of private apartments grouped round a family bedroom. These apartments were placed together and expressed as a separate family wing within the plan. The family apartments were linked to the main block, which was itself grander in style and taste. A third unit in the plan was the servants quarters which were placed out of the way of the main activity of the house, away from the everyday view of the country house owner or casual guest. At Camperdown these were situated along a side of the courtyard and were expressed on the exterior by being smaller in height relative to the main house. A logical sequence was laid down progressing from the dining room to the family apartments which would allow the country house owner both to entertain in considerable style, and at the same time retain a high degree of privacy.

This privacy was enhanced as Burn ensured that the service quarters were grouped, together with secondary rooms and smaller family

Plate 36
Camperdown House,
Tayside, 1824.

rooms for the junior members of the household, along one side of the office courtyard.
Private staircases for the family rooms were
included, and private entrances to the family
suite were designed.

The sources of these developments in
country house planning lay in the equally
prevalent and important castellated and
Gothick designs which all combined to break
down the stranglehold of classicism and
purely symmetrical planning. (The Gothick
taste reflected a romantic impression of Gothic
architecture, in reality it was light, insubstan-
tial and a confectionery immitation of true
Gothic principles and designs. This was why
this decorative style was called 'gothick' to
distinguish the period from the medieval

Figure 26
*Camperdown House,
Tayside.*
Principal floor plan: The
public rooms form one unit
along the length of the
house, on the southern
facade, to the west another
distinct unit was formed by
the family apartments.

Gothic styles which dominated architecture from the eleventh to
sixteenth centuries.) Examples of the native tradition of Gothic architecture could be seen in Scottish Post-Reformation churches, and some
elements of this tradition were to survive in the designs of William
Bruce at Holyroodhouse, and in country houses such as Thirlestane
Castle. In addition some of the origins of the style and its eventual
popularisation were to be found, somewhat ironically, within the work
of the Adam brothers, and the work of Robert Adam in particular.

One of the first castellated houses in Scotland was **Inverary Castle**
[plate 37] designed by Roger Morris (1696–1749) for the third Duke of
Argyll. The castle was begun in 1744, and was an ambitious building
conceived with a rigid symmetry and given a mock-Gothic dress. The
inspiration behind the use of the startling mock-Gothic castellated style
may be traced back to two closely interlinked sources. Firstly there was
the requirement laid down by the Duke of Argyll which spelled out the
desire for a castle. There was a perceived need by the Campbells of
Argyll to create a mansion reflecting their family power and wealth,
but to create a mansion in an archaic style so as to reflect their traditional position as Scottish landowners and political leaders within the
nation. The style was in one sense an emotional response re-affirming
the fact that the Dukes of Argyll were an important Scottish family who
were conscious of being Scottish. This lead the Duke of Argyll to
approach Sir John Vanburgh to provide designs for a castle at Inverary.
The initial sketches provides by Vanburgh echoed that
architect's own interest in castelled forms – his own house in London
was treated as a castle but built out of local brick. Vanburgh's interest
in fortifications and castles made him a natural choice for the Argylls to
engage to put their own ideas on paper. These designs are the second
source of inspiration for Inverary Castle. The Duke of Argyll eventually
opted for Roger Morris as the architect, but in truth Morris followed on
from where Vanburgh had led – so closely in fact do the outlines and

Plate 37
Inverary Castle, Argyll,
1744.
The garden facade of
Inverary Castle.

skylines of each architect's drawings, plans and designs mirror each other.

The building was altered after a fire in 1877, but the original plans and elevations to Roger Morris' design were published in William Adam's *Vitruvius Scoticus*. The house was planned [figure 27] about a central saloon, which rose almost two full storeys above roof level. At each corner of the house large circular turrets were placed to accent the concept of a castle. The principal floor was entered via a bridge across a dry 'moat' – this dry moat itself held the basement storey which was occupied by extensive servants quarters. To the left and right of the entrance hall on the piano nobile were the dining room and the drawing room. Leading directly off from the hall was the saloon, and beyond it a long gallery. The interior was typical of contemporary taste, being based upon the enfilade and axis of honour concepts with appropriate state bedrooms for important guests located on the principal floor as well. The interiors were decorated in the classical style, and the house was based on a clearly symmetrical plan. What was certainly atypical of the period was the choice of exterior decoration and style. This castle aspect was further reinforced through the use of green-grey stone for the construction of the building. The sombre colour reinforced the image of a strong and defensive seat of a powerful family.

The house was completed by 1758 under the supervision of William Adam and his successors John and Robert. They provided designs for the planned town of Inverary just on the outskirts of the Castle, and for the bridges which linked the estate to the new military road from Dumbarton. Robert Adam would also provide drawings and schemes for the remodelling of the interior in the 1780s.

This castellated Gothic style of Roger Morris may have inspired the

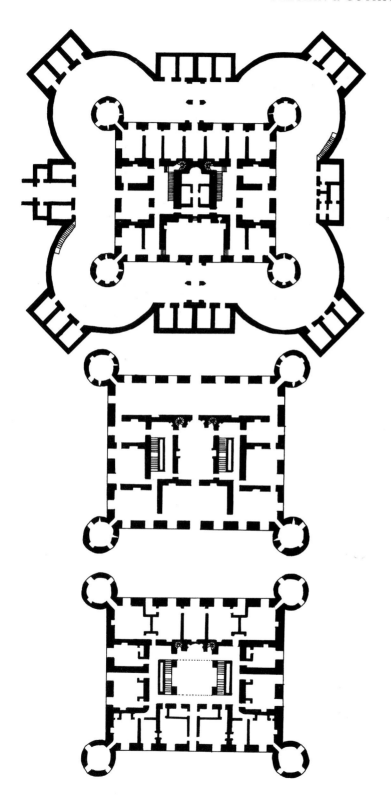

Figure 27
Inverary Castle, Argyll,
1744.
Top: Basement floor plan,
containing all the domestic
offices.
Centre: Principal floor
plan.
Bottom: Second floor plan.

Adam brothers to design **Douglas Castle** [plate 38] for the first Duke of Douglas between 1757 and 1761, for it was very similar in appearance and plan – although it rose four storeys over the basement whereas Inverary rose only two. It was designed as a 'U' shaped building[figure 28], but was not completed fully as the brothers had intended. The sequence of rooms as they led from the entrance hall matched those at Inverary Castle. Also matching were the pointed, almost Gothic, arched windows, a specific design feature that Robert Adam did not repeat in his later castles.

The contrast between this castle style and Adam's own castles can be clearly seen when looking at **Mellerstain House** [plate 39] built by Robert Adam between 1770–78 for the Hon George Baillie. The facade was, in this case, articulated with oblong windows topped by stone mouldings. No pointed arch windows were included in this house. Robert Adam designed the central block of seventeen bays to create an 'E' shaped arrangement which would join the two existing (and supposedly William Adam) wings of the house together to form one continuous and unified facade [figure 29]. For an Adam design the house was unusually long and thin, really only three bays in depth, but Adam skillfully hid this by linking the house to the wings with a small two block service stair and anteroom. This gave the house the appearance of both depth and greater stature, and created a forecourt in front of the mansion [plate 40].

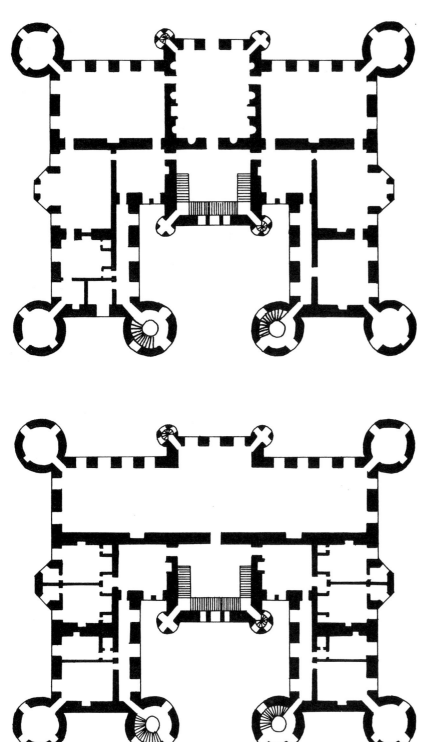

Figure 28
Douglas Castle, Strathclyde.
Top: Principal floor plan;
the service stairs are
contained in the turrets.
Bottom: Gallery floor plan,
with bed chamber wings.

Plate 39
Mellerstain House, Borders, 1770.
The garden facade – the gardens slope gently down to a lake.

Plate 40
Mellerstain House.
The entrance facade. The ground is at a higher level to the front of the house, typical of Adam's approach to the design of servant quarters.

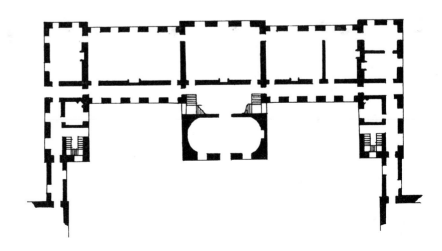

Figure 29
Mellerstain House.
Plan of the principal floor.

As the site at Mellerstain inclined downwards to the south the base-ment storey was at ground level to the gardens at the rear of the house. Unusually, at the very top of the house, above the entrance block was a gallery running the breadth of the house. This was a clear echo of his father's placing of libraries out of the general household melee. In this instance the purpose of this room at Mellerstain House is not readily apparent, though it may have been intended as a gallery and viewing room from which broad vistas over the estate could be obtained. In this way the gallery would have actually formed a traditional feature and acted as a link to the history of earlier Scottish country houses.

Plate 41
Culzean Castle, Strathclyde, 1777.
The formal rhythm of Adam's classical castle facade.

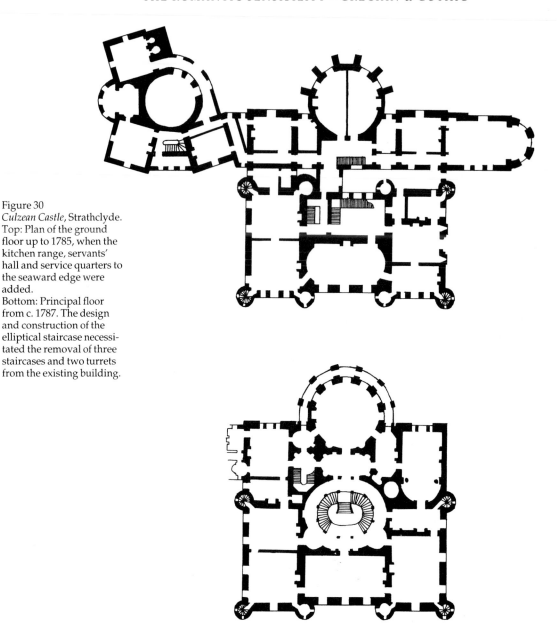

Figure 30
Culzean Castle, Strathclyde.
Top: Plan of the ground
floor up to 1785, when the
kitchen range, servants'
hall and service quarters to
the seaward edge were
added.
Bottom: Principal floor
from c. 1787. The design
and construction of the
elliptical staircase necessi-
tated the removal of three
staircases and two turrets
from the existing building.

Adam may also have begun building castellated buildings to
economise on the costs which his patrons and clients would be
expected to pay for a new mansion. His detailed classical compositions
and interiors were a significant drain on the resources of many a
prospective country house builder. Perhaps, as an alternative, Adam
struck upon the idea of a cheaper method of providing a country house
this time cast in simpler clothes, with all the sumptuous decoration and
classical show reserved for the interior. The facades of such simpler
mansions would be articulated through the massing of the building,

through the roof lines, and through the regular rhythmic placing of the window openings, rather than through expensive detailing and the carving of stone elements on the exterior. Adam in these castle houses made full and extensive use of the classical language and tradition in which he was trained, and in which he believed, to encompass and to draw into the architectural establishment the concept and image of the castle within contemporary ideas of country house design.

His later castles developed to become just as extravagant statements in form, plan, and style as many of his other classical buildings. **Culzean Castle** [plate 41], built from 1777–90 for the tenth Earl of Cassillis was perhaps the most significant and largest of all his castle style commissions. Culzean involved the extensive remodelling of an earlier 'L' shaped castle. Robert Adam regularised the castle along the lines of a strictly symmetrical plan [figure 30], but then added an asymmetrical kitchen wing, centred on a circular brew house. From the entrance courtyard of the house the geometrical order of relieving arches, classical detailing and window shapes prevailed. On the seaward side the house, perched as it was on the clifftop, took on the most romantic of outlines [plate 42]. Adam was in essence designing very much within the classical language and tradition – the servant wing though asymmetrically built abutting the main house was designed as a symmetrical unit in itself. Each of the varied units of Adam's plan for Culzean Castle betray their symmetrical heritage, and detail in essence Adam's own preference for designing within a clas-

Plate 42
Culzean Castle, Strathclyde, 1777. The romantic seaward facade, the north elevation.

Plate 43
Oxenfoord Castle,
Midlothian, 1780.
A typical Adam castle,
with Victorian additions.
(RCAHMS)

sical symmetrical format. Though the castle had an asymmetrical element this was achieved almost by chance. The parts of the whole were all based upon simple geometric patterns and the governing rule was symmetry. Adam's asymmetry (introduced by the siting of the brew house) was very tentative indeed.

The remainder of Adam's castles – such as **Oxenfoord** [plate 43] for Sir John Dalrymple, **Dalquharran** [figure 31] for Thomas Kennedy, or

Airthrey [plate 44] for Robert Haldane – all fall into the same category of classical houses designed with a castellated exterior dominated by classical motifs. Dalquarran, in particular, was another fine example of Adam's castle style. He designed the castle for the family of his niece. It was to overlook the ruins of an earlier castle of the same name, and as at the nearby Culzean, was to be perched atop a cliff. Dalquarran was however inland, away from the eroding effects and ravages of the seaborne elements. In silhouette Dalquarran was almost like a Roman fort, and perhaps Adam was again drawing upon the experiences of his continental trip to extend the range of his designs.

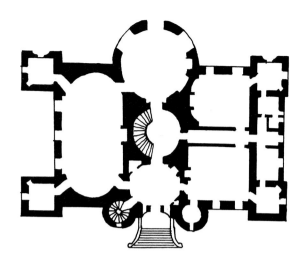

Figure 31
Dalquarran Castle, plan.

Adam did allow his imagination to almost run riot when dealing with a castle, Airthrey was designed along a semicircular plan; Adam designed triangular houses as well. Robert Adam did express a greater sense of freedom in his castle style designs towards the later stages of his career that was not apparent in the designs which he would produce for a classical mansion. Perhaps a variety of forms was essential to encourage his clients to accept such novel forms, or perhaps – just as likely – his clients were anxious to promote a country house which was both original and individual. This riot of variety reflects both contemporary demand for the unusual, and Adam's ability to respond to it. Where Adam led with quirky interpretations and pastiche of the past, others were to follow with sincere and archeological recreations.

Plate 44
Airthrey Castle, Central,
1790.
View of the entrance facade
of the Adam castle before
additions of 1890.
(RCAHMS)

CHAPTER 5

The Early Nineteenth Century, Scots Gothic and Jacobethan

W ith the turn of the century Scottish architecture entered a further new phase. Society had been rapidly changing from primarily an agricultural base to one dominated instead by the new and developing industrial centres and commercial businesses. The new rising class of industrialists and financiers aimed to join the social elite, to confirm their position and to translate money and wealth into power. In this search they followed on from where others had already led in the emulation of the landed classes in fashionable taste and the construction of many differing kinds of building. As before the country house was still the established prime source of power and position within the social elite. These mansions remained and continued to be centres of political power; their occupants represented the elite of society, and the country house cycle of weekends, dinner parties and entertainments was developed for the dual purpose of light amusement and the more serious business of political agreements, negotiations and industrial strategies. Furthermore, since the eighteenth century, if a prospective candidate wished to stand for election to Parliament he had to be able to fulfil specific landownership requirements – this was yet another reason why land was at a premium and treated as an important commodity, and why country houses were seen as symbols of position and prestige.

It is important to note that the turn of the century saw further changes to the apparent pace of society itself. Whilst the later eighteenth century had by and large been a reaction against rigid formality and had witnessed the introduction of greater personal freedoms, the nineteenth began with a reaction against the social whirl which the previous decades had themselves promoted. No longer a furious circle of engagements the social scene became less structured and more relaxed. House parties gradually became more informal and typical days involved quiet, relaxed pastimes.

For example, a typical day at a country house at the start of the 1800s began with breakfast at around nine o'clock. After this, guests and their hosts amused themselves by reading, walking in the gardens of the estate, or by playing cards. The most popular room was perhaps the library, which acted like another informal sitting room or drawing room. Dinner had moved from five o'clock in the afternoon, which was the common hour in the 1750s, to six-thirty or seven o'clock in the evening. Previously, dinner had been followed by cards, tea, and conversation with a light supper at ten o'clock before bed at midnight. Now because the men of the house would go shooting or hunting after breakfast, and because the ladies would be left at the house to enjoy the gardens and the walks in the grounds of the house, a new meal was introduced for the first time – called luncheon. This new meal was intended to occupy the ladies left behind at the house until the return of the men. Dinner became the strongest residual element of formality around which the day was structured. Appropriate evening dress would be required. Supper was retained, but now at eleven o'clock instead of ten. The expected time for family and guests to retire would still be midnight. Servants would have to be up at work before the family rose for the day, and they could be expected to work well into the night as well.

Little change in this broad schedule was to occur in terms of the real everyday functions of the country house for the greater part of the century. The main developments were in terms of the physical operating technology of the country house, the evolution of country house planning and the treatment of the exterior of the buildings themselves. The early nineteenth century would see the elevation of Gothick taste (the elegant and charming eighteenth century imitations of medieval detailing with little real regard for medieval principles) from a few sugar candy affectations into full blown Gothic restorations and recreations. But the style was gradually moving towards a firmer foundation based upon the beginnings of archaeological researches. The starting point for these Gothic buildings was found within the works of Robert Adam and mansions such as **Scone Palace** [plate 45].

Plate 45
Scone Palace, Tayside, 1803.
View of the garden facade.

Scone Palace was built for the third Earl of Mansfield by William Atkinson (1773–1839) in a picturesque Gothic style. It was the first of many such houses to be styled by Atkinson in this manner. Scone Palace was designed about a double courtyard plan, with the private family apartment forming a quite separate and clearly distinct unit within the house. These private apartments were placed adjacent to the main public block of the house which contained the important function rooms. The difference between the two purposes of the private apartments and public wing as expressed by the plan of Scone Palace was also apparent in the execution of the exterior of the building in that the two wings were not treated as identical mirror images of each other. Atkinson's plan carefully considered the privacy of the country house owner, and was one of the first to use the expedient of a recognisable family wing to create that much prized privacy.

In addition, though Atkinson could be regarded as an unoriginal and somewhat insensitive architect at times, at Scone he did consider carefully the history of the house and the significance of the site. For example, in building the house Atkinson retained the old eastern and southern ranges of the existing property to reinforce the air of tradition and the real antiquity of the building; he altered the main entrance on the eastern side so that from the gatehouse the new state door was clearly in a direct line of vision, emphasising again through this axis the linkage of the old and the new; and finally within the house the entrance hall led into an octagonal vestibule, from which followed, on differing faces, both the long hall and the old gallery, giving the overall impression of a cloister. The plan combined the feelings of historicism (with the house being given over to a rather monastic style construction

Plate 46
Crawford Priory, Fife, 1810.
View of the main facades of the mansion.
(RCAHMS)

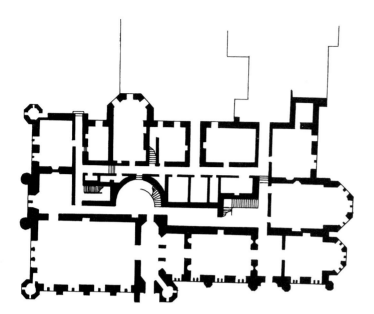

Figure 32
Crawford Priory.
Plan of the principal floor c.
1810, adapted by the
author from an original
plan in the care of the
(RCAHMS)

on the exterior) and those of daily comfort in one. By 1811 the house
was to cost the Earl of Mansfield £60,000, and he thought that it more
than answered the expectations which he could have had of a mansion
or of his architect.

Another such individualistic and innovative mansion was **Crawford
Priory** [plate 46, figure 32] begun for Lady Mary Lindsay in 1809 by
David Hamilton (1768–1843). In 1811 Lady Mary changed her architect
and opted for the services of James Gillespie Graham. One architect
had clothed an earlier eighteenth-century house in confectionery
Gothick, while the latter added substantial rooms to the rear of the
house and the stable courtyard in both ecclesiastical Gothic and castellated Gothic. Crawford Priory was self-consciously idiosyncratic and
determinedly unusual. Both houses had little direct and immediate
effect on other properties or wider stylistic influence as such, and were
in essence reflections of the somewhat unique and individual tastes of
their patrons.

Perhaps the most important of these Gothic houses in terms of influence exerted upon the future of Scottish country house design came in
1814 with the construction of **Dalmeny House** [plate 47] for the fourth
Earl of Roseberry. Up until that date the Earls had lived in the family
seat of **Barnbougle Castle** on the shores of the Firth of Forth. The
family had considered building a new mansion (to the designs of
Robert Adam; a triangular castle style building), but they were eventually forced to evacuate the house due to its age and proximity to the
waters of the Forth. When the sea water flooded Barnbougle Castle the
Earl set about the business of constructing a new suitable imposing
mansion for himself and his family. He requested drawings from the
most notable architects of the day and selected a design by William
Wilkins (1778–1839). Wilkins had offered Lord Roseberry the choice of

Plate 47
Dalmeny House, East
Lothian, 1815.
View of the main facades of
the house.
(Joe Rock, photographer)

options between either a Grecian design or a Gothic one. Roseberry plumped for the Gothic plan because it was the very latest taste (James Wyatt had just exhibited the drawing of **Fonthill Abbey** for Lord Beckford at the Royal Academy Exhibition of 1813) and because Lord Roseberry was very well aware of the fact that the design could affect a change in the architectural history of Scotland.

The house was built along an asymmetrical plan [figure 33]. A compact family wing was placed to the left of the main entrance hall and on the right following an 'L' shaped formation, the public rooms were ranged to allow views overlooking the Forth. The public rooms were linked to each other in a natural ordered progression, and they were also linked to a main corridor which transversed the length of the house. What was immediately noticeable from the plan of Dalmeny House was the organisation of these public rooms as they ran from the dining room through the ante room, the drawing room and finally to the library. This particular pattern and arrangement would virtually become the norm for country house planning for the remainder of the century. It was a systematic organisation of connecting and related

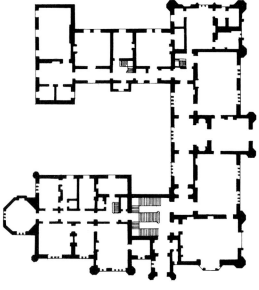

Figure 33
Dalmeny House, East
Lothian, 1815.
Principal floor plan. Lord
Roseberry's private family
apartments form a distinct
separate unit. The public
rooms interconnect in a
logical sequence.

units that, in working effectively became increasingly accepted and almost unchallenged in terms of popularity and efficiency. The farthest reaches of the Dalmeny House were occupied by the servants quarters. These quarters also included the basement storey which contained the kitchens. Access to the main public rooms or the private apartments of Dalmeny House for the servants was channelled through a series of servants stairs and corridors. In this way the daily work of the servants could be done efficiently without the owners themselves actually having to encounter the staff working in the house during the course of their duties. The servants work was done without being seen to be done.

The development of a separate service wing by 1814 was not however a novelty. There was already in existence at some country houses an identifiable wing or a separate floor which would contain the sleeping quarters of some servants. By 1810 these servant wings would in general terms also include the kitchens, the servants day rooms and servants eating rooms. The servant rooms as a whole at this time were usually taken up from out of a basement storey, so that this could be used solely for cellars, if they were required, or, more usually, so that the principal floor (the piano nobile) could be lowered to ground level. This lowering of the floor of taste – the principal floor – reflected the desire of country house owners to be able to walk unhindered from house to garden. It also reflected a desire to remove the servants to a more clearly defined space all of their own, away from the main house, and separated from the country house owner. These changes were made possible by the introduction of sophisticated and complex bell systems. These bell systems allowed servants to be called to particular parts of the house, rather than have them waiting ready in attendance. It was only in the 1780s that such technology was exploited to any great degree – and this was to satisfy the growing demand from country house owners for privacy from their staff.

The effect of this new technology was to permit and thereby to further encourage the development of asymmetrical planning, as there was a greater desire to separate off servants into a distinct wing, cutting them off from the main house almost completely. As country house owners began to appreciate the pleasures of their landed estates more – for hunting and entertaining, and for the simple joys of the country life, so they began to spend more time, sometimes as much as six months at their country house. They believed that life in the country house should in many ways reflect the pastoral beauties of life in the country. As part of this idealised life servants were a necessity, but they were, somewhat like the children of later generations, to be seen and not heard.

Wilkins' plans for Dalmeny, and later at **Dunmore Park** [plate 48] for the fifth Earl of Dunmore (who like Lord Roseberry was a member of the Society of Dilettanti), mirror the requirements of the emerging nineteenth century country house classes. Indeed at Dunmore (built from 1820), Wilkins extended the 'L' plan of public rooms which he had developed at Dalmeny so that it ran completely along two facades of the house [figure 34]. This was achieved by the inclusion of an office room for Lord Dunmore, and a billiard room. This 'L' plan arrange-

Plate 48
Dunmore Park, Central, 1820.
South-east facade, as drawn by the architect.
(RCAHMS)

ment of public rooms and the compartmentali-
sation of the various functions of the country
house, together with the use of the Gothic style
was in essence to form the basis of country
house planning for the remainder of the
century.

This method of planning was taken up and
perfected by the most prolific country house
designer of the age – William Burn. A stag-
gering 180 commissions, remodellings and
complete country house designs were
executed by Burn during his working life. In
terms of planning what William Burn offered
his clients was simple – he offered them
privacy. Additionally he was prepared to
compromise over detail, plan and style to
satisfy his client's wishes and their pockets.
His main rivals in the market of producing
country house designs in Scotland were James
Gillespie Graham and William Henry Playfair.
These two architects were to complain bitterly
and frequently at Burn's continued and
prolonged success, for example Playfair was
to write in 1841 that:

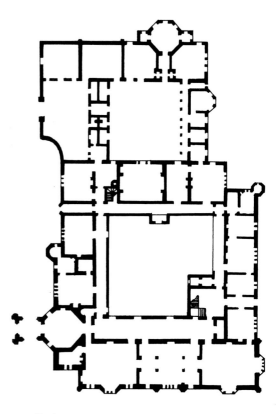

'Burn meantime carries everything before him, generally however
creating horrid blots on the landscape wherever he is employed,
and is again becoming more purseproud and ostentatious and
overbearing than ever. His utter want of genius is only to be
equalled by his copious supply of impudence'. [17]

Figure 34
Dunmore Park, Central,
1820.
Principal floor plan – with
the inclusion of the billiard
room, Lord Dunmore's
offices and the communi-
cating hall the public
rooms form into an 'L'
shape. To the top of the
plan separate courts were
provided for men servants
and women servants.

William Burn was the son of an architect builder of passing distinction.
In 1808 he was in the busy architectural office of Robert Smirke, a
London based Scot. By 1810 he had returned to Scotland to begin his
own practice. His early designs displayed none of the thought, planning and control which would occupy the remainder of his career.
Within ten years Burn was to establish the formula which was to ensure
his success as an architect and designer of major country houses.

Burn knew his patrons and clients, he understood their needs, and
was keenly aware of the privacy which they sought and held so dear.
He also knew how they wished to regulate and control their own daily
existence. He sought to satisfy these needs through the provision of
logical sequences of rooms, planned with economy and constructed to
meet the complex considerations of privacy and the varied questions of
effective domestic service. Broadly speaking, his attitudes to the planning of the domestic offices, the family wing, and the main block of a
country house developed out of the conditioned experience of the late
eighteenth century. They followed on from the Palladian, Neo-

Palladian, and Gothic experiments with a new, almost zealous thirst for privacy. Privacy was to be attained at the expense of formality and it would encourage the development of new attitudes to the domestic, social and working conditions and to the surroundings of both the country house owner and his servants. Burn, above all other considerations, aimed at providing privacy for his clients. This can be seen on the most simple of levels in that he did not publish drawings of houses designed by him – in this way their owners could feel safe in the knowledge that their house was completely their own. In addition he seldom built his houses above two storeys to allow the family apartments access to the gardens, and to preserve a relationship between the house and its grounds.

Because Burn designed so many country houses from his Edinburgh offices, and later also from his London office, it would be tempting to consider his method of design merely a formula, with little room for invention. It is true that William Burn found a ready solution to the problems of country house design that suited those most concerned with the process – that is to say the country house owners themselves. His popularity was evidence enough for that. However the sheer volume of his work does show that the variety of ideas were lacking and room shapes, room placings, and interpretations of room functions were repeated again and again in his various country house plans to meet the demands of the sheer volume of work before him. In this way Burn was perhaps almost derivative, but his discovery of a successful formula which satisfied the demands and constraints of country house

Plate 49
Carstairs House,
Strathclyde, 1827.
View of the entrance front
of the house. (RCAHMS)

life was significant in itself.

Burn's first mature plan and house was that at **Camperdown House** [plate 36, figure 26]. Here the private apartments were planned starting from a family bedroom – rooms progressed outwards from this family bedroom to separate suites for the master and mistress of the house, with their own bedrooms and dressing rooms. This private apartment was expressed on the plan and the elevation of the house as a separated wing, and was linked en suite to the main body of the house. The same features can be said to appear at **Carstairs House** [plate 49], designed in 1821 for the MP Sir Henry Monteith, or at **Riccarton**, built for Sir William Gibson Craig in 1823. The only really significant difference between these houses and Camperdown, apart from the actual detailing and specifics of their plans, was the style of architecture employed for the exteriors. Camperdown was in the Grecian taste, whereas both Carstairs and Riccarton were in an English Jacobean mode (sometimes called Jacobethan to distinguish this revival style from the historically correct period). Both Carstairs and Riccarton had Jacobean shaped gables and corbelling. The logic of the plan of each house was expressed visibly on the exterior of the buildings (through differing roof heights and levels of decoration) in a manner which the superficially symmetrical Camperdown could not fully accommodate.

Figure 35
Ratho Hall, Midlothian, 1824.
The mechanics of a William Burn mansion depend upon connecting corridors running parallel to the main rooms.

For the facades of **Ratho** [figure 35] in 1824 Burn added new elements of Tudor battlements to the English Jacobean decoration. Only the elevation of the southern facade of the house retained a fully symmetrical arrangement. This country house plan was a prototype for many subsequent designs. The entrance to the house was placed on the east front of the mansion. The three principal and important rooms ran along an axis to the south, with the office court and servants wing running to the north. This was a smaller country house for the architect, as the finances to complete a planned larger residence were not in the end available from the client.

Burn, in 1829, was the first architect in Scotland to design in the Scots Tudor style. This style was based on the romantic writings of the extremely popular novelist Sir Walter Scott and the ecclesiastical architecture still in use by contemporaries which gave the architect source information from which to draw inspiration. Sir Walter Scott was amongst those in the forefront of a movement calling for the development and introduction of a purely Scottish style of architecture, one that would reflect both the romantic history of the nation and its native strengths and vitality. His own house at **Abbotsford** [plate 50] had been designed by William Atkinson between 1816 and 1823, and was a touchstone for both the Romantic and Gothic sensibilities. Its asymmetrical plan and variety of room shapes, which were expressed on the exterior through numerous bay window projections and differing

heights and levels, was typical of the period. Indeed these experiments and evolutions in style and planning set the tone for country house designs in the decades to follow.

The castles of James Gillespie Graham follow in this developing asymmetrical school of design. Though Gillespie Graham was to build thirty-six country houses, and consider himself to be a friend and fellow traveller of the arch Goth of the nineteenth century – A.W.N. Pugin – the majority of his work can be said to be rather repetitive and even run of the mill. **Dunninald House** [plate 51, figure 36] and **Edmonston Castle** [plate 52] are two good examples of his overall style. The plans of both mansions bear the telltale signs of a Gillespie Graham house. They are almost symmetrical, but with the placement of a large circular tower at one end of the facade set the whole building on a rakish asymmetrical bent. The public rooms were organised in an 'L' shape, about the main hall, and ran from

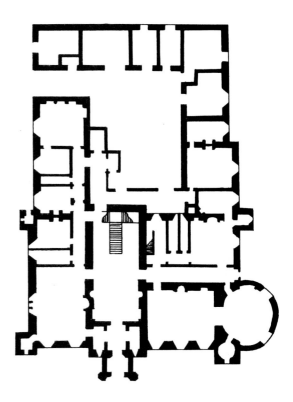

Figure 36
Dunninald House, Tayside.
Principal floor plan.

Plate 50 (opposite, above)
Abbotsford House, Borders,
1816.

Plate 51 (opposite, below)
Dunninald House, Tayside,
1823.
The muscularity and
vertical force of the round
tower is offset by both the
octagonal tower and the
low horizontal block of
private apartments.
(RCAHMS)

Plate 52
Edmonstone Castle,
Strathclyde, 1815.
View of the house from the
gardens. (RCAHMS)

dining room, drawing room to the library (which occupied the lower floor of the end circular tower). Though Gillespie Graham was serious in his intention – the Gothic style was important to him and his interiors were to bristle with a more authentic Medieval flavour than previously encountered in the work of almost any other architect – the execution of the exteriors was particularly coarse. He was perhaps aiming for a secular variant of a monastic style of architecture in the hopes of accenting the picturesque quality, this merely added to the building's unscholarly appearance.

Pugin is a very significant figure and his mention is important as the myriad of ideas expressed in his writings radically changed the course of architecture, and also design in the applied arts, throughout the nineteenth century and succeeding generations. Agustus Welby Northmore Pugin (1812–1852) was a prolific designer, theorist and architect. Responsible for furniture designs for Windsor Castle and most of the fabric of the Palace of Westminster Pugin's importance to nineteenth century architecture and his legacy was his writings and thoughts on the importance and superiority of Gothic architecture. In 1836 he published *Contrasts*, a fighting book, with a rabble-rousing text and illustrations to show the reader in direct and simple images his message and to reinforce the justness of his cause. Pugin had emerged from a growing and vital tradition of English writers and philosophers, antiquarians and gentlemen amateurs all fascinated by and interested in the promotion of Gothic architecture – whether as a curiosity or as a distinctly national and British style. Research into the Gothic past and its architectural remains was being started all across Europe. Coincidentally at the same time new building magazines and publications were founded (1834, *Architectural Magazine*; 1837, *The Civil Engineer* and *Architect's Journal*; 1843, *The Builder*). The various publications would allow the Gothic revivalist message to be fostered and promoted. Allied to these developments was the establishment of the professional institutions such as the Royal Institute of British Architects (1835). The debate and activity generated by all the main sources of research and the enthusiasm generated by its many supporters would be tapped by Pugin to extol the virtues of the Gothic style and the Medieval society from which that style had originally evolved. Pugin believed that Gothic architecture was the only true and natively English style of architecture. Only Gothic architecture was both honest and Christian, and classicism (in any of its forms) was essentially foreign and pagan.

Pugin approached architecture with a religious zeal and fervour, believing that a return to first principles would lead to the saving of British architecture from shameful experimentation and the mere application of decoration for decoration's sake. Pugin believed that the honesty of a building would be revealed in its materials, in its construction, and in the work of craftsmen upon the fabric. Pugin called for a style of architecture that reflected the history and the integrity of the nation. He believed in thorough historical research to provide both inspiration and precedent – much in the manner that the Greek Revivalists had achieved only a few years before. Like them Pugin's publication of his ideas made them both popular and current in the imagination of the public. Pugin's thoughts upon architecture led to a groundswell of opinion throughout the profession and amongst the public in general against superficial decoration and applied styles in favour of honest construction methods and the development of architecture suitable to the locality of the building. His ideas were to dominate the course of architectural practice in one form or another for the remainder of the nineteenth century.

The theories of Pugin became part and parcel of the Gothic Revival, and they became part of the continuing search for a basis for the establishment of a National Style. In 1841 Pugin published his *True Principles of Pointed or Christian Architecture*. In this book he furthered his contention that Gothic architecture was Christian, and therefore English, by an impassioned defence of the Medieval way of life. Indeed the book was also a call for the resurrection of the medieval way of life, a call for human relations and social structures to be based on a more human scale and for society to be more equally balanced and organised. He had already attacked Classical architecture in his 1836 work *Contrasts* by somewhat romantically comparing the contemporary conditions of the poor in a now industrialised Victorian England, with an idealised view of their conditions under the benign monasteries of Medieval Britain. Here he had proposed that Gothic architecture was morally superior because it was Christian, and concerned with elevating the minds of those who inhabited such buildings to proper and higher thoughts. These ideas were extended in *Principles* by Pugin's attack on both senseless over-decoration of Gothic forms and their debasement through unsympathetic or simplistic copying of out-of-context archaeological features for a 'Gothic' effect. He proposed a theory of good design to change the whole situation – though he knew himself that he was as guilty of poor design as anyone else.

The principles of his theory of design were threefold. Firstly, features which were not necessary to 'convenience, construction or propriety' should not be adopted. Secondly 'all ornament should consist of enrichment of the essential construction of the building'. Finally, the 'external and internal appearance of a building should illustrate, and be in accordance with the purpose for which it was designed'. These principles emphasised the central theme of honesty of construction. Pugin aimed to ensure that the Gothic Revival was not merely superficial or rote copying of the past, but an honest working within the Gothic spirit through a fuller understanding of the Gothic vocabulary.

Just as the Neo-Classical revolution had sought an Arcadian dream of a national style throughout the eighteenth century, so now it became the turn of Gothic sources to attempt the same. The period at the beginning of the nineteenth century in Scotland was neatly summarised by John Dunbar, who encompassed the main drifts and changes in taste and style when he wrote:

> 'So far as country houses were concerned, Scottish architects and patrons from the first showed a decided preference for the castellated and Gothic styles, and by the beginning of Queen Victoria's reign native romanticism had inspired, in revived Scottish Baronial, an appropriate northern variation of its own'. [18]

CHAPTER 6

Scottish Baronial

The Scottish Baronial style evolved out of the whole gamut of ideas, theories and themes that existed in the early nineteenth century. Its origins were in the romantic sensibility of Sir Walter Scott and also the strict moralising and architectural theory of A.W.N. Pugin. The beginnings of the style could be seen in the work of William Burn and David Bryce, his younger assistant and later partner. From English Jacobean and Tudor styles Burn made the small evolutionary leap towards the development of the innovative Scots Tudor and Jacobean. He adapted his knowledge of the English styles to a new taste, reflecting a stronger Scottish tone. The Scottish Baronial style was an attempt at reintroducing into Scotland a version of historical vernacular types based on the few surviving examples from the Baronial period. This began at **Milton Lockhart** [plate 53], designed in 1829–36 for William Lockhart. This house was possibly the first major country house designed in the revived Scottish vernacular style. William Burn provided Lockhart

Plate 53
Milton Lockhart,
Strathclyde, 1829.
The west, entrance front.
(RCAHMS). Permission to
reproduce Hamilton Public
Libraries.

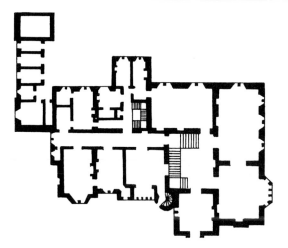

Figure 37
Milton Lockhart,
Strathclyde.
The public rooms are
crowded in a compact unit
on the principal floor.

with a robust house, neatly proportioned with mullioned windows and heraldic shields to enliven the exterior. The house and its plan [figure 37] follow all the needs of country house design required by Victorian owners. In this respect the house followed the Burn planning pattern developed to meet those specific needs.

Privacy to both the Victorian country house owner and planner was the central and vital ingredient. It was one of Robert Kerr's most valued qualities when he wrote on the subject of *The Gentleman's House* in 1865. The only way to achieve the quiet comfort that country houses were intended to secure and achieve was to design for privacy:

> *'It becomes the foremost of all maxims, therefore, however small the establishment that the servant's department shall be separated from the main house, so that what passes on either side of the boundary shall be both invisible and inaudible'.* [19]

On top of this the family would have

> *'free passageway without encountering the servants unexpectedly... the outdoor work of the domestics shall not be visible from the house... (and further) it is equally important that the walks of the family shall not be open to view from the servants' department'.* [20]

These were the conditions of privacy upon which the Victorians insisted. Country house plans tried to organise and regulate every duty and function within the daily routine of the mansion. This would be done with as much detail as possible and as much efficiency as possible. Country house owners expected their servants to complete their work without being seen – as W.R. Lethaby explained:

> *'it was the affectation of that time, that work was done as if by magic, it was vulgar to recognise its existence, or even to see anybody doing it'.* [21]

Above all, designers of country houses tried to ensure that the owning family would have privacy and that the servants would have enough space – sometimes this was barely the minimum of space and personal freedom – in which to complete their daily chores.

To achieve these requirements numerous physical, social and organisational structures were applied and set within a country house at the earliest planning stage. Though the servant wing was a necessary

Plate 54
House of Falkland, Fife, 1839.
The main block of the
house.

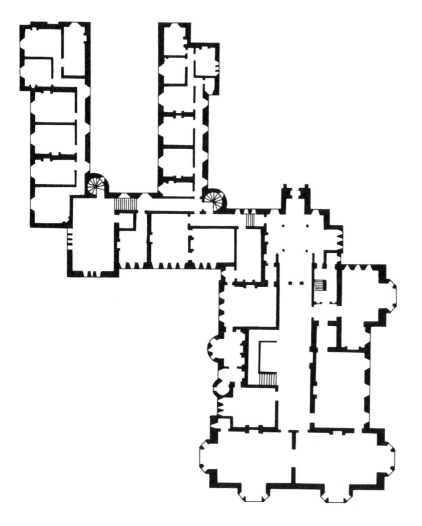

Figure 38
House of Falkland, Fife.
Principal floor plan – the
two wings at the rear were
service rooms, male staff to
the east range and female
staff to the west. The public
rooms permitted an 'L'
shape within the plan, as
did the private apartment.
The house was remodelled
in the late 19th century.

adjunct to family apartments and public rooms, and even sometimes much larger than the main block of a country house – as at **House of Falkland** [plate 54, figure 38], for example – it was never allowed to appear so. The facade of the main house was decorated and positioned in such a manner as to make it abundantly and immediately clear to the viewer that 'the one part of the edifice is as the superior and the other is the inferior'. [22] [plate 55]

Reinforcing the divisions and stratifications in society could be achieved in architectural terms by simply screening the domestic offices with architectural features added to the main house – billiard rooms or conservatories were frequently used for this purpose – or by screens of trees and shrubs. (A good example of this was the building of a conservatory block for Largo House during the mid 1850s which partially obscured the servants quarters from view.) Another method achieved similar results by building the main block on one level and the servants block on a lower level (in some ways this was an adaptation of already existing planning methods and country house types). This slope method was very popular. Not only was it economical but it fulfilled the needs of visual appearance, it did not allow the servants to view the family's private walks and gardens, and it did not necessitate the use of basement offices (which were felt to be depressing for the staff). The servants wing of the house would be generally less detailed, plainly decorated, and built to smaller proportions.

The segregation of servant and family continued into detailed physical restrictions within the interior of a country house. The servants had their own back stairs and corridors for communications throughout the

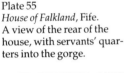

Plate 55
House of Falkland, Fife. A view of the rear of the house, with servants' quarters into the gorge.

Plate 56
Pollock House, Strathclyde,
1747.

house, to complete their tasks unseen. There was the 'green baize door'
– the point at which the house and the servants wing would meet – a
symbol of the division and the point at which work was done by magic
on one side, and daily work was very highly organised and structured
on the other.

These were the general conditions, the ambience, which surrounded
the conception of a country house plan. As for the plan of the servants
wing itself this depended on how many servants were required by the
family. The average number of servants was rarely less than ten per

household, and rarely more than fifty (**Pollock House** [plate 56] had on average forty-eight indoor servants). The size of a servant wing was determined by the required number of servants, rather than by the number of servants available. At this time domestic service, though difficult and hard work, was considered something of a superior position compared to other positions of employment on offer.

In both the main house and the servants' wings the Victorian architect attempted to segregate the sexes, reflecting the strict moral climate to which serious attention was paid – though in reality this may often have been no more than lip service. Male servants would have single bedrooms in one part of the servants quarters, and maidservants would be expected to share a bedroom in another part. Quite often male and female were separated on different floors or in different accommodation blocks of the house. This prescription applied equally to unmarried children or guests staying at a country house, where a bachelor wing was often to be found. In the main house this segregation led also to separate wings or floors for male and female family members or guests.

This tendency to split rooms into masculine and feminine domains was not new to the nineteenth century. The dining room had long been considered a masculine preserve, as too had the library and the billiards room. Drawing rooms, morning rooms, and sitting rooms were all the feminine arena. This attitude extended itself during the Victorian era to all aspects of the plan of the country house.

Most important for any Victorian country house was the positioning of the kitchen in relation to the rest of the house. This room had to be given the most advantageous location – it had to be far enough away from the dining room and the main house so as not to let cooking smells stench out the house, but close enough not completely to freeze the food. Invariably however food did arrive chilled, and a new service room was added adjoining the dining room to heat up the food before serving. As Kerr was at pains to point out:

> 'the transmission of kitchen smells to the family apartments shall be guarded against; not merely by the unavailing interposition of a passage door, but by such expedients as an elongated and perhaps circuitous route, and interposed current of outer air, and so on'. [23]

Grouped about the kitchen were the servants hall and the work rooms which were the engine of the country house. The housekeeper and the butler were in charge of this territory. They had to ensure the smooth running of the household and only they would receive full instructions from the family to pass on to particular servants. Sometimes needless subdivisions of labour were identified and an endless series of rooms was called for to ensure that everything would have its place, and only one place at that! The whole hierarchical system of designing a country house along these lines was open to over specialisation and a concentration upon too much detail – especially in the servants quarters.

Plate 57
Floors Castle, Borders.
The entrance facade.

In the main house the public rooms and the functions of entrance hall, dining room, and drawing room did not really change. The library became a more important room in many houses. It acted more akin to a sitting room, and did not necessarily require the presence of any books at all in a room to call that room a library. Perhaps the greatest addition to the country house was the rebirth of the medieval hall as a dramatic entrance motif and eventually as a general entertainments room and lounge. The hall had been reintroduced in tandem with the medieval revival which swept across the nation. Such halls were not too popular in Scotland, being mainly an English Gothic Revival feature.

What, however, was popular in Scotland was the evolution of the Scottish Baronial style. The medieval revival encouraged Scottish architects to record, to research and attempt to recreate those styles of the Scottish Renaissance that Sir William Bruce had abandoned almost two centuries before. At **Floors Castle** [plate 57] for example, William Henry Playfair reclad the plain classical William Adam house in new Scottish vernacular and Jacobean dress in 1837–45 for the sixth Duke of Roxburgh. The inspiration for the new style was to find written form in the researches of R.W. Billings, who followed the trend now firmly established of publication to further expound and popularise the surviving examples of true Baronial fragments. Later, in 1888–92 Ross and McGibbon would publish *The Castellated and Domestic Architecture of Scotland*, which became a reference book and source of ideas for those designing in the Baronial manner.

David Bryce was the real innovator in the development of the Scottish Baronial style that spread so rapidly across both the nation and the world beyond. His early houses, such as **Tolcross House** [plate 58], dating from 1848 and designed for the industrialist James Dunlop, were very much in the mould formed by his partner William Burn. The house was built in a confident Neo-Jacobean style, though it did entertain a few restrained and minor sub-Baronial details – for example the crow stepped gables.

Seacliffe House [plate 59, figure 39] was designed in 1841 with a festooning of Baronial detailing from crow stepped gables to bartizans

Plate 58
Tollcross House, Strathclyde, 1848.
View of the mansion, the main entrance is to the centre of
the house. (RCAHMS)

Plate 59
Seacliffe House, East Lothian, 1841. The entrance facade.

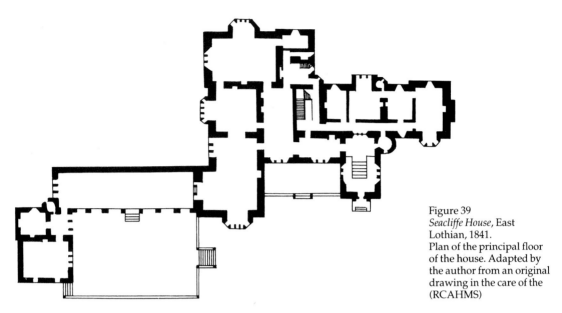

Figure 39
Seacliffe House, East
Lothian, 1841.
Plan of the principal floor
of the house. Adapted by
the author from an original
drawing in the care of the
(RCAHMS)

and endless corner turrets. The same can be said of **Ormiston Hall** which Bryce designed in 1851 for Sir Alexander Wilkie. The construction of both houses was surprisingly similar, despite their difference in size. Bryce, like Burn was a prolific architect, much in demand. He would design extravagant, elegant and costly buildings for his clients, and then scale these down omitting details and whole rooms until his

Plate 60
Balmoral Castle, Grampian, 1855.
Entrance facade and
approach.

patron's pockets could match the design before them. In this manner, though Bryce ranks amongst the finest of the Scottish Baronial architects, with some of the most interesting and intriguing designs to his credit, he also appears one of the more repetitive. At **Birkhill** designed in 1857–59 Bryce reconstructed an earlier house into a Baronial mansion. He virtually doubled the size of the main house, and in the process removed the original servants quarters – thereby creating the necessity of building a new office court. All in all, despite Birkhill's prominent position overlooking the Tay estuary, the detailing employed was rather routine – Bryce had opted for romantic effect rather than historical accuracy.

The most typical Scottish Baronial mansion must be that of **Balmoral Castle** [plate 60], built in 1855 for Prince Albert and Queen Victoria at their own expense as a family retreat from the stresses of London life. The house was partially designed by the Prince and also by the Aberdeen architect William Smith (1817–1891). The massing of the house is unusual, and the rhythm of the fenestration, the bay projections and the roof line again rather repetitive. At the same time the very essence of the Scottish Baronial style was held within the simple massing of form and the repetition of detailing or similar features within the same facade. This occurred to notable effect at Balmoral [plate 61]. The style of the house has been somewhat unfairly dubbed 'Baronial Schloss' as, perhaps because of the influence of the Prince, a Germanic air could be said to envelop the property. The house design was really quite modest in terms of the other buildings that were being erected all over the country in the mid years of the century; thus reflecting both the middle class tastes and modest resources of the monarchy at the time.

Much larger, and completed during the same period were the remodelling works carried out by the Duke of Sutherland at **Dunrobin Castle** [plate 62, figure 40]. These were executed mainly by the celebrated architect Sir Charles Barry and then later W. Leslie between 1844 and 1850. The Duke of Sutherland had previously employed Barry at his English estates remodelling **Trentham**

Plate 63
Dunalistair House, Tayside,
1852.

Hall in Staffordshire. The style employed here, though classed broadly as Scottish Baronial, had heavy French overtones, particularly in the roof lines and the elongated turrets.

The Baronial style continued to be used with frequency into the dying days of the nineteenth century. **Dunalastair House** [plate 63] was designed and built in 1852, encompassing an earlier smaller building as part of the newer house. The entrance facade of the house was unusual in that it was symmetrical, being centred on a rather French chateau-like tower and turret. The house was built for General Sir John MacDonald to overlook a spectacular wooded viewpoint, in a respectable Highland setting.

The partnership of Burn and Bryce split with an acrimonious dissolution and the younger architect was to prove himself more adept at exploring what, after all, was the home market to both architects. Burn's Baronial was more restrained, but retained the key features of the style; that is to say a prominent square based tower rising above the general height of the main house, crow stepped gables, corner turrets and bartizans, corbel stone mouldings and detailed carved stonework, with dormer windows breaking the roof line of the house.

At the same time as new Baronial country houses were being constructed older, and already somewhat decayed properties were beginning to be resurrected and brought back into use. This was all part of the Medieval revival, and part of the scholarly researches into the history of the nation. One such property was **Kellie Castle** [plate 64]. The original house had been remodelled by Sir William Bruce, and contained a number of Bruce's most exuberant plasterwork ceilings. In 1878 the Earl of Mar agreed to lease Kellie Castle to Professor Lorimer

Plate 64 (opposite, above)
Kellie Castle, Fife, 1603.
Main entrance facade,

Plate 65 (opposite, below)
Skibo Castle, Highland,
1900. (RCAHMS)

108

Figure 41
Skibo Castle, Highland.
Plan of the principal floor.

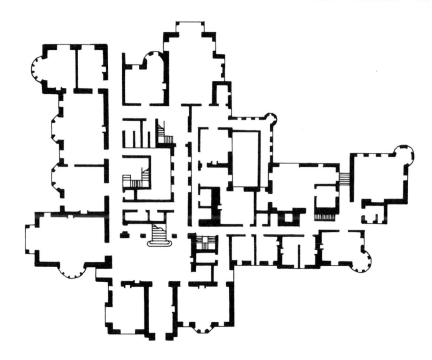

on a thirty-eight year lease, and to make the building weatherfast for
his new tenants. The castle was to become the Lorimer's summer residence. Whether they would have wanted to completely refurbish and
extend the castle along the lines of contemporaries was never a question which arose for serious discussion – neither the financial where-
withal, nor the inclination to remodel the property took root in the
Lorimers. What they aimed to do was resurrect a house which had
almost been derelict. This concept was to have important repercussions
for the final years of the century, and the careers of country house
designers into the first years of the twentieth century.

At **Skibo Castle** [plate 65, figure 41] the former steel magnate
Andrew Carnegie spent £100,000 from 1900 to 1903 to transform a
small house on an existing estate, bought in 1898, into a large mansion
suitable for entertaining Royalty and his own friends in the Liberal
party Government. Andrew Carnegie was the richest man in the world,
having sold his US Steel Corporation for £100 million. His own modest
tastes were such that at Skibo he found the house too grand, and had a
smaller mansion constructed for himself and his wife, not far from the
Castle, elsewhere on the estate. The pink granite of Skibo dominated
the skyline. Close to the house in the grounds a vast marble and glass
swimming pool was built, with the most up to date technology for
heating the sea water with which it was filled. When the swimming
pool was not in use as such it could also double as a ballroom:

'... *Huge electric arc lamps and chandeliers glittered*

overhead... Tubs of evergreens were spread along the walls, and festoons of coloured paper chains and bunting hung overhead... Mrs Logan's dance band from Inverness played in the balcony, varied by bagpipe music for Scottish reels and so forth, highland Scottische ... played so harmoniously by the castle piper'. [24]

Skibo Castle emulated royal living at Balmoral Castle in retaining its own piper. This grand political house was designed by the Inverness architects Ross and MacBeth. It was one of the last great Scottish Baronial houses to be built.

CHAPTER 7

Towards a Free Style

I n the later years of the nineteenth century architectural thought and
practice in Scotland were dominated by the legacy of William Burn.
To a very large extent country house planning and design followed his
example in the creation of specialised rooms connected by long lines of
communication and numerous back stairs, main stairs, private corridors, servants corridors and other endless passages. This particular
kind of house relied on high staffing levels, and the owners of country
houses would expect many people to want to work for the family in
such a country mansion. Cheap labour was in relatively abundant
supply. In Scotland only the new industrialised cities of Glasgow and
Dundee were of a size to be a potential drain on the pool of manpower
or a threat to the equilibrium of wages.

The introduction of new technology did influence country house
design to a certain extent towards the close of the century. The bell pull
system for calling servants was almost universally in use. Central
heating systems and full plumbing were considered essential for the
most modern of houses, and, where possible, all country houses were
being updated and brought up to new standards of comfort and taste.
Electric lighting was introduced in country houses first at **Cragside**
[plate 66] in 1872. Cragside was built in Northumbria for Lord
Armstrong, the armaments manufacturer, by the architect Richard

Plate 66
Cragside, Northumberland.

112

Norman Shaw in his English vernacular style. One of the earliest houses in Scotland to be lit by its own electricity supply was **Balruddery** [plate 67], where the owner, the Liberal MP Martin White, was able to persuade his friend the inventor Marconi to adapt the house to this end in 1892.

Plate 67
Balruddery House, Tayside. View of the house.

Norman Shaw, one of many pupils of William Burn, was perhaps the most famous architect of that generation which succeeded Burn and Bryce. What is notable is that many of the most important of these designers in this succeeding generation did not build in Scotland, or at least did not design country houses there. (One house in Norman Shaw's massive English vernacular style was **Keil House** [plates 68, 69], designed in 1870 by the Glasgow architects Campbell, Douglas & Sellars for J.N. Fleming – a director of the City of Glasgow Bank. The house was dominated by a four storey tower, which looked over broad sweeps of roofing, together with the occasional half-timbered gable

Plate 68
Keil House, Argyll, 1870. View of the main facade of the house. (RCAHMS)

113

Plate 69
Ruins of *Keil House*, Argyll.

and mullioned windows. The impression was in the manner of Cragside, without Cragside's dramatic site or superior architect.) This dearth of building in Scotland may be due to the fact that England was the central stage of country house building, and that it was to England that foreigners came to observe and marvel at the workings of the whole class system – of which, no doubt, the country house was seen as the epitome within the hierarchical structure that was British society. One example of this foreign interest and research was the work of Herman Muthesius, a German diplomat, who advocated the values and the designing flair of British architects in his book *The English House*.

New ideas, fashions and styles were also adopted. These in many ways emerged out of the existing traditions and philosophies of architecture and design. They were yet another metamorphosis in style. Just as the family of Professor Lorimer renovated the decayed Kellie Castle for its summer residence so others either did the same or built entirely new castles. **Penkill Castle** [plate 70] and the **Old Place of Mochrum** are but two examples. Penkill was a favourite haunt of the important central figures within the Pre-Raphaelite Brotherhood, Christina and Dante Gabriel Rossetti. It was remodelled to meet with their aesthetic tastes, while at the same time keeping its fifteenth century character. The Old Place of Mochrum was also a fifteenth century castle, but this time brought back to life by the Marquis of Bute. He restored the castle to its medieval splendour using the contemporary 'Arts and Crafts' ethics originally espoused by William Morris, and then taken up with great gusto by all quarters of polite society. The Marquis was a true Medievalist following in an archaeological tradition. His aim in the recreation of the past was in many ways a meditation upon an ethical life – he attempted (much as Pugin had in his writings and works) to create for himself mansions where the honesty and integrity of the Arts and Crafts aesthetic had real meaning, rather than merely being the superficial application of a style.

The Arts and Crafts movement beginning in the 1870s was a turning point in country house design. The ideas central to the movement were echoes and developments of the theories and words of Pugin from the

114

1830s. Just as Pugin had praised the honesty of Gothic architecture William Morris, the greatest leader of the movement, praised the integrity of craftsmen making furniture or otherwise involved in the applied arts. He decried the general poverty and squalor endured by the mass of the population, which he could see all about him. He argued that their sufferings were the direct result of the industrialisation of the country. Morris despised the use of machinery to produce items. They, he believed, had removed the connection between man and the creative process; machines could mass produce items, and these would be devoid of unique individual and human touches. Any item could be subject to the industrial process and could therefore be debased, reduced to crude imitations of great individual works, and would involve at each stage of production the exploitation of the worker. Industrialisation created standardisation and commercialism destroyed the individuality of craftsmanship. In addition products could be made anywhere and transported over great distances – no recognition would therefore be given to differing local traditions or materials; only the market was important, only the market and that which would sell in it.

Morris' answer to this dilemma was to return to basics, to reject the use of the machine and its culture, in favour of traditional craftsmanship, traditional methods, and traditional tools and materials. Importance was placed upon the creation of items which were honest

Plate 70
Penkill Castle, Ayrshire.

Plate 71
Melsetter House, Orkney,
1898. (RCAHMS)

Figure 42 (opposite, above)
Melsetter House, Orkney.
Plan of principal floor, the
house was designed about
two sides of the entrance
courtyard.

Plate 72 (opposite, below)
Earlshall Castle, Fife, 1898.
View from the topiary
garden.

to the materials from which they were made – for example, items made from wood should exhibit the strengths and delicacies which could be achieved by the substance, and they should show off the material to its best advantage. As for architecture, the local traditions and building materials should be respected, to try and match the new building with the tone of its surroundings. Architecture should appear both natural and a part of the landscape, not something imposed upon it to dominate and control. A building should be constructed using the materials to their best advantage and with honesty and integrity.

116

In terms of country house designs as a general rule the Arts and Crafts movement had a greater influence upon the interior and the applied arts than upon the plan or the exterior of a mansion. There are exceptions to every rule. One mansion was **Melsetter House** [plate 71]. Designed in 1898 for the Birmingham businessman Thomas Middlemore, Melsetter House provided Scotland with her first truly Arts and Crafts country house. Middlemore had decided to retire from manufacturing and purchased 40,000 acres upon which he eventually decided to remodel an existing laird's house. The architect he chose for this task was William Richard Lethaby (1857–1931), one of the leading lights of the Arts and Crafts movement. Lethaby provided a plan from his London office, but when he arrived on site, Lethaby quickly altered his vision of the house. The plans were revised as he recognised that the original laird's house could and should be incorporated into his design. The house which was created was large and informal, replete with traditional elements [figure 42]. The new house was built along traditional lines and employed traditional methods of construction. Its walls were of sandstone rubble and then covered in harling. The harling did not fall straight to the ground, where it would have accumulated dirt, nor did it reach right into the corners of the facade, where it would be vulnerable to accidental chipping. Instead it met the ashlar trimmings which in turn also accented the lines of the house. The plan of the house followed a typical 'L' shape, with the masculine rooms of smoking room and gun room situated at some distance from the main public rooms. In his extensive works at Melsetter House Lethaby also remodelled the outbuildings and altered the steadings at the rear of the house to create a rose garden.

The most important Scottish architect within this new Arts and Crafts tradition was Sir Robert Lorimer, who grew up at Kellie Castle. Lorimer brought together in

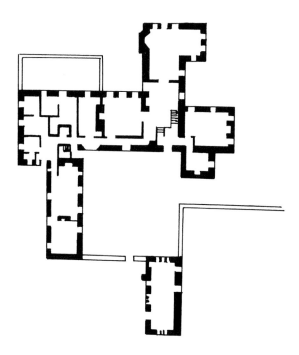

his architecture all the strands of the nineteenth century together with the technological developments in construction and design in his architecture. His first major house was the restoration of **Earlshall Castle** [plate 72] in 1892 for the Perth industrialist and collector W.R. MacKenzie. Lorimer completely renovated the castle as a family home for MacKenzie and as a showpiece for the display of MacKenzie's excellent collection of antique furniture and tapestries. These twin features of antiques and tapestries, and of Lorimer providing a design for a mansion to act as home to a collection of antiques and a wealthy family, were to crop up again and again in the work of Lorimer in later years. At Earlshall Lorimer provided the house with a recreation of a Scottish Renaissance walled garden modelled on those at **Edzell Castle** [plate 73], which Lorimer was often to visit.

At Earlshall Lorimer is rumoured to have met one of his most important clients and a close friend (until an irreconcilable argument drove the two men apart in 1914) – Sir William Burrell. Through Burrell

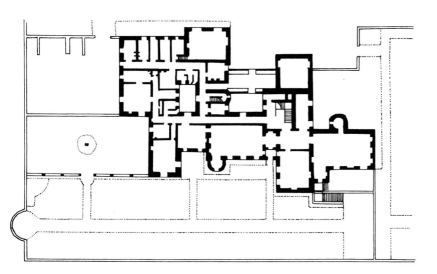

Figure 43
Rowallan, Strathclyde.
Plan of the principal floor.

Lorimer was to be introduced to some of the most significant art and antique collectors and potentially important clients that any young architect could ever have wished to meet. Burrell was to be Lorimer's most important friend, until their argument over the remodelling of **Hutton Castle** (bought by Burrell to house and display his own impressive art collection).

Lorimer saw himself as designing within both the Scottish and the Arts and Crafts traditions. His first new commission to provide a complete design from scratch, rather than a remodelling of an existing structure, came from an MP, Cameron Corbett, at **Rowallan** [plate 74]. The house designed by Lorimer retraces the Baronial Revivalist path on the grand scale. Surprisingly the main rooms were placed on the first floor (the piano nobile), in the manner of sixteenth and seventeenth century precedents [figure 43]. The gardens were reached via a terrace in front of the drawing room.

Cameron Corbett later, full of praise for the house which had been designed for him, introduced Lorimer to Sir Andrew Noble so that he too would have a Lorimer house. Sir Andrew Noble was a very successful businessman, being chairman of the armaments and industrial company started by Lord Armstrong. The house which Lorimer designed for Sir Andrew Noble was **Ardkinglas** [plate 75], which was somewhat in the same mould of Lord Armstrong's Cragside but in a Baronialist taste. Here again Lorimer placed the main public rooms on the first floor [figure 44]. The ground floor was given over to the servants quarters and the general business rooms of the house. An entrance porch led into a hall and beyond to the grand staircase, from which access was gained to Sir Andrew Noble's office and the billiards room. On the first floor a saloon was the first public room encountered after climbing the stairs. A grand corridor led to an upper hall and the dining room. What was unusual about the plan was that there was no separate drawing room, and that the saloon was intended to double for

Plate 73 (opposite, above)
Edzell Castle and gardens.

Plate 74 (opposite, below)
Rowallan House,
Strathclyde, 1902.
(RCAHMS)

Plate 75
Ardkinglas, Argyll, 1906.
The garden facade.
(RCAHMS)

Figure 44
Ardkinglas, Argyll
Plan of the principal floor.

this purpose. The house was replete with the most up to date conveniences – Lorimer provided the estate with a hydro-electric dam and power station from which the electricity for the mansion was generated. Ardkinglas was designed in 1906.

Whilst Lorimer was continuing to design in the Baronial mode – the sixteenth century was his favourite period – other designers and patrons were requesting different styles to reflect their own tastes, and no single style dominated the country house market. James Younger, a scion of the brewing family, in 1902 asked Paul Waterhouse to provide designs for **Mount Melville** [plate 76]. The house was to replace an earlier mansion by James Gillespie Graham and was completed in the Jacobean Chateau mode, accenting the French influence in the Auld Alliance. The house was subdued in its detailing. This gave it both the touch and air of established respectability and was, apparently, the conscious choice of the nouveau riche owners who did not wish to overstep contemporary unspoken rules of social etiquette. Unusually the house was completed in red sandstone, a building material not local to the St Andrews area. The stone for Mount Melville was imported at some expense, being delivered to the building site by rail and by cart.

At the other extreme of both opulence and style was the recreation of a great Adam mansion in impeccable Edwardian taste in 1901. **Manderston House** was originally a three storey high mansion with a mansard roofed second floor. Sir James Miller, the owner, had married into one of the most aristocratic of English families in 1893 when he took the Hon Eveline Curzon, daughter of Lord Scarsdale, as his wife. Lady Miller's home until her marriage was **Keddlestone Hall** in Derbyshire, perhaps the greatest Adam classical house in England. Sir James wished

Plate 76
Mount Melville House, Fife, 1908.
The entrance facade.

Plate 77
Manderston House, Borders, 1890.
The entrance facade.

to make his bride feel comfortable in her new home and set the architect John Kinross (1855–1931) to redesigning Manderston [plate 77].

Kinross was a Glaswegian architect of some reputation, having successfully renovated parts of Falkland Palace earlier in his career. At Manderston he completely changed the atmosphere of the house by giving it an almost severe classical air. The exterior was given a restrained facade with a two storey portico which doubled as a porte cochere. In the interior the model of Adam taste and style was adopted everywhere – the house was in tandem with a contemporary Adam revival, and was a style adored by Edwardian designers. The hall was perhaps Manderston's most special feature, it recreated the atmosphere of that at Keddlestone without being a direct copy. Kinross had turned to the surviving Adam drawings and designs made for Keddlestone. He employed the same colour scheme and motifs for the hall at Manderston as Robert Adam had used over a century earlier for the hall at Keddlestone. The Adam interiors at Mellerstain House, only a few miles away, provided similar source material from which Kinross drew inspiration.

The classical taste was much in evidence at **Symington House** built by Andrew Prentice. The house was completed in 1915, just as the clouds of war had descended over Europe. Symington was one of the last of the large country houses to be built, reflecting the changes which were affecting country house designs and plans. The style of the house, with its Neo-Georgian classicism, was a mask to its very modernity.

123

Plate 78
Hill of Tarvit, Fife, 1906.
Garden facade

The estates grounds included a chauffeur's lodge and purpose built garaging for cars. This last feature was unusual.

At **Hill of Tarvit** [plate 78, 79], for example, another Lorimer mansion, the architect converted the existing stable block of the early mansion of Wemysshall to garage space for the house. The original house of **Wemysshall** had been designed by Sir William Bruce in 1696. The 1904 house had been bought by the financier Frederick Sharp as his new residence, and as a place to display his art collection. Frederick Sharp was involved extensively in the development of business in America, he was also a director of a railway company, and owned three ships with Sir William Burrell. The house was not really suitable for either purpose (as a family home or as a place of display), and Sharp asked Lorimer to remodel the property. Lorimer had met Sharp at Earlshall at a party organised by Lorimer's first client MacKenzie.

The Hill of Tarvit [figure 45] created by Lorimer was designed around the collection of furniture and tapestries made by Sharp from 1896 onwards. The exterior of the house was harled in a traditional Scottish manner. The style of the house was difficult to pinpoint. It was reminiscent of the small classical house which it had displaced, and also resonant of French architecture because of the use of large French windows which led onto the garden terracing. The inspiration for these windows was the collection of French Louis XV period furniture which Sharp wanted exhibited to the very best. The house, as designed, was of a very manageable size, with four public rooms running along the garden front from drawing room, great hall, library, and eventually to

124

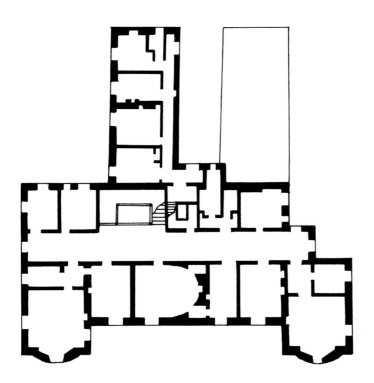

Figure 45
Hill of Tarvit, Fife.
Top: First floor plan – all
the family bedrooms open
off one corridor.
Bottom: Principal floor
plan.

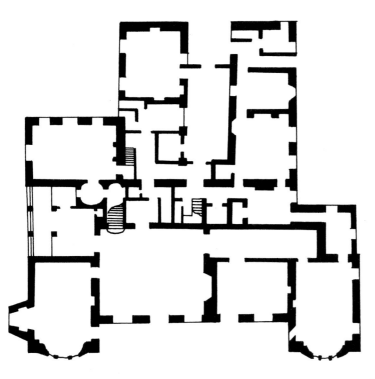

the dining room. Leading off the hall, through a double archway, were the main stairs. At the turn of the first flight of these stairs was the billiards room. Being at half height and a mezzanine floor the billiards room also led out onto the garden which rose in a slope at the rear of the property.

Hill of Tarvit was typical of the new smaller, more modest country houses built at the close of the century and in the first years of the twentieth century. In plan it was quite simple – a corridor ran the length of the house and all the main public rooms were arranged on the south front, so that they would make best use of the warmth and daylight from the sun. The servants quarters were usually much smaller and more compact. All modern conveniences, from running water to central heating and electricity were installed to make the houses comfortable. The staff at Hill of Tarvit rarely numbered more than twenty four in total, and this included thirteen outdoor staff required to look after the woodlands and gardens of the estate. In addition Hill of Tarvit was typical in the size of its landed estate in that the house itself could not really be supported by the estate of 1,600 acres. The house was kept in style by the financial and business activities of its owner.

With the industrial expansion agriculture had lost its premier position as the sole supporter and guarantor of the dominance of the country house. Where extra sources of income were not available houses would be sold, or they would be abandoned to decay. One odd example of this process was **Formakin House** [plate 80, figure 46] built for John Holms in 1906 by Lorimer. Once again the house was to be

Plate 79
Hill of Tarvit, Fife, 1906.
Entrance facade, showing
servant quarters to the rear.

designed purposefully around the collection of tapestries and antiques in Holms' possession. The tapestries determined the very room sizes as planned by Lorimer. When Holms' partner in his Glasgow stock-broking office absconded, leaving Holms to bear the full financial responsibility for a series of rumoured illegal deals, Holms paid out over £100,000 overnight in 1912. Holms had spent a considerable fortune already on his collection and the purchase of neighbouring parcels of land to create an estate. His nature was not that of a man ready for capitulation. His financial position was such that he was able to pay off all debts, but nothing more.

His great baronial mansion was roofed, the structure made weather tight, but it was never finished. Johnnie Holms believed that given time and patience and a great deal of acumen his financial position would improve and he would be able to complete the mansion. Holms had a smaller farmhouse on the Formakin estate in which he lived, and remained the rest of his days beside the dream home which he was never able to complete. He would still use Formakin, even in its half-finished state. Occasional dinner parties would be held at the house. A makeshift kitchen would be organised so that the meal could be cooked. A table was set up in the dining room where the servants would serve the meal to the somewhat bemused and astonished guests whom Holms had invited to view his home. The collection, which Holms had spent many years amalgamating, was set up in the rooms of the house as if the mansion was fully occupied. When he died Holms' house was sold, and would remain unoccupied and incomplete. Most

Plate 80
Formakin House,
Strathclyde, 1908.
View of the house from the sundial garden.

Figure 46
Formakin House,
Strathclyde.
Top: First floor plan.
Bottom: Principal floor
plan – the main rooms
were formed to house a
private art collection.

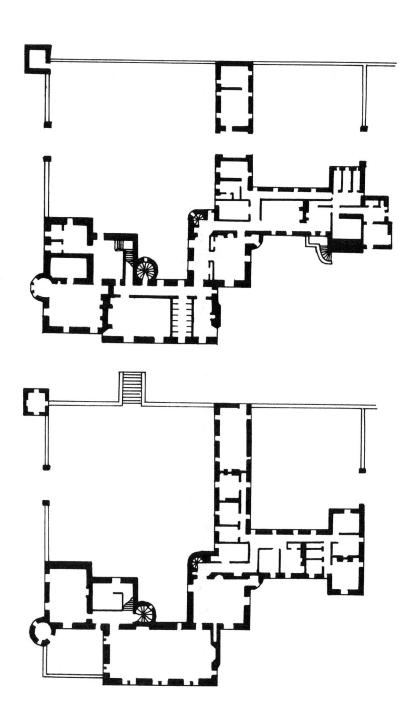

Plate 81 (opposite, above)
Formakin House,
Strathclyde, 1908.
View of the unfinished
great hall at Formakin.

Plate 82 (opposite, below)
Formakin House,
Strathclyde.
View towards the entrance
courtyard, which bears a
strong similarity in feel and
articulation to Kellie
Castle.

Plate 83
Kellie Castle, Fife.
View from the walled
garden.

of the art collection which he had spent years amalgamating was bought at auction by Sir William Burrell.

Formakin stands both a monument to a great idea and the individualistic dreams of John Holms, and also to the passing of an age. After the First World War the age of the country house was in decline as the society which had supported it as the epitome of achievement was to disappear in a social revolution. The house also stands as a monument to the building techniques of Sir Robert Lorimer. At Ardkinglas Lorimer used modern methods of construction to complete a massive structure in as short a time as possible – his client was seventy years old and wanted to see his house complete before his dotage. These methods were left exposed when building stopped so abruptly at Formakin: steel reinforcing rods poke through floors, brickwork was left bare of decoration, and the central heating channels left exposed in the cement floors – indeed in the main hall there is a touching reminder of the building of the house where the footprints of a dog, embedded in the wet cement as the animal ran out across the room before being called back to heel, are still visible today [plate 81]. The exterior of the house, the appearance of solid stone construction was in reality a deliberate sham. The house was built of brick and reinforced concrete. Lorimer knew that as an architect he was designing a house in the style of the past, the whole house, in and out, and the gardens and grounds were one large conceit [plate 82, 83].

CHAPTER 8

The Decline of the Scottish Country House

*W*hilst country houses through the process of everyday occupation were constantly being altered, modified, rebuilt and generally added to for over two hundred years, the arrival of the twentieth century saw a new phenomenon: the death knell was apparently beginning to toll. The status of the country house as the pinnacle of society and social achievement was challenged, first through social change, then financial circumstance, and finally through political necessity.

The first destruction of a major country house of national, if not international, importance was that of **Hamilton Palace** in 1919 [plate 84]. The seat of the Dukes of Hamilton and Brandon, Hamilton Palace was perhaps the largest private house in the country, and indeed one of the very few to truly deserve the title 'palace'. After sales of furniture, paintings, and effects in 1882 to cover extensive family debts the house was somewhat of a vast empty white elephant. It was revived temporarily as a Naval Hospital as part of the War effort, but with the end of hostilities in 1918 the house fell quickly into disuse. No longer needed as a family home, and far too large to maintain even for institutional usage, the passing of Hamilton Palace was noted with real regret in 1922. There was however no concerted and organised attempt to preserve this important example of cultural and architectural heritage for future generations. That was not the mood of the times, and such

Plate 84
Hamilton Palace,
Strathclyde.
The garden facade.

ideas would only become popular a decade or so later – eventually resulting in the founding of the National Trust for Scotland in 1931. All that remains today of Hamilton Palace is the Ducal Mausoleum, a bricked up gate lodge, and the Hunting Lodge of Chatelherault – all subject to subsidence through extensive mineworkings [plate 85, 86].

The root causes of the passing of Hamilton Palace (one of approximately five hundred country houses between 1900 and 1970 to follow a similar ruinous route) lie mainly in the architectural taste and social premise which formed the basis of their designs and plans. The financial difficulties of the Dukes of Hamilton, and many other families like them, merely serve to confuse and compound the inherent complications of country house planning and life. Hamilton Palace was a significant signpost on the road marking the decline of not only the country house but also of a way of life.

That decline was a direct result of the social changes occurring throughout the nineteenth and early twentieth centuries. Whilst accidental damage and fire – such as at houses like **Penicuik House** (1890) [plate 87] or **Cambo House** (1878) [plate 88] – could devastate a property, it was the prevailing social and economic conditions at the start of the twentieth century which would decide the fate of many a country house.

The most important social change throughout the nineteenth century had been the increased stratification of society, and thereby the

Plate 85 (opposite, above)
Hamilton Palace,
Strathclyde. The coach-house with the domed mausoleum behind.

Plate 86 (opposite, below)
Hamilton Palace,
Strathclyde. The 'sleeping lion' on the ducal mausoleum.

Plate 87
Aerial view of *Penicuik House,* Midlothian, 1760. The stables (top left) were converted into a house after fire devastated the mansion. (RCAHMS)

Plate 88
Cambo House, Fife, 1879.
The entrance facade.

development of a recognisable class system for which Britain became famous. Architects went to such extreme lengths to keep family and servant segregated that they created country houses with elaborate, and highly specialised, class dependent compartmentalised solutions. These country houses employed a great number of servants for all the various detailed domestic functions. Additionally, if all the outside staff and their families were counted then the country house was a substantial community often reaching as many as one hundred people. Even country houses without a large working estate or agricultural base, would have a significant level of servants (at least ten) to keep the property running smoothly. Though the worlds of master and servant were kept artificially apart in the name of privacy, the two classes were actually overlapping and almost totally inter-dependent on one another.

A constant supply of cheap labour was therefore essential. The Victorian specialisation of labour in the country house applied across the board in the division of servant's duties. The staff were the oil that lubricated the cogs of this particular machine and they kept the whole running efficiently.

If the Industrial Revolution had allowed some people to climb the social scale through inventions, enterprise and wealth made in 'trade', it also widened the opportunities for that class who traditionally worked upon the laird's estate. The growth of industries such as the jute mills of Dundee, or the shipyards of the Clyde acted as magnets upon the migrant labour force. Industrialisation gradually appeared to provide marginally better wages and working conditions to tempt some of the 'servant class' away from their traditional employment. Whilst such industrial jobs carried no greater security nor even the free board and lodging that came with a domestic position, they did allow greater personal freedom and financial independence. On top of this a wave of emigration in the 1870s and 1880s increased the competition in the labour market. This all contributed to the perceived 'servant problem' at the end of the nineteenth century.

In 1916 an enquiry by C.V. Butler for the Women's Industrial Council, focusing on the employment conditions for domestic servants noted that:

> 'During the first two months of the war many servants were dismissed, and there was a temporary over-supply of under-house-maids and lady's maids. Munitions work and other new occupations for the women have absorbed all of this over-supply, except in the case of a few upper servants, and have made the shortage of servants more acute than before'. [25]

The greater part of these researches had been completed before 1914.

The servant problem became a constant topic for discussion in contemporary periodicals and magazines. Though the problem may

Plate 89
Dalquharran Castle,
Strathclyde, 1757.
The ruins of Dalquharran.

Plate 90
Dalquharran Castle,
Strathclyde, 1757.
Front entrance, with view
through to ruined interior.

have had greater significance south of the border, it evolved into a constant lament that 'one cannot get the staff today'. Though the problem was not actually as severe as it was first thought to be at the time it is important to realise that servants were at a premium, and therefore an expensive commodity. At the same time good servants were essential to the running of the country house.

The two decades between the World Wars saw a loss to Scotland of 46 houses of note. Houses such as Isaac Ware's **Amisfield** (1928), Robert Adam's **Walkinshaw** (1928), his **Dalquharran** [plate 89, 90] and **Douglas Castle** (1937)... these are all now only names and records. Numerically these losses were not as severe as in England or in Ireland, but they were severe by any standards. Scottish estates, which had their special place in British social life through their hunting and shooting holidays, and through their romantic attachments, were treated as valued properties. When a shooting estate or lodge was lost during the inter-war period it was treated as a calamity – yet little was done to really address the situation. Indeed the middle classes were now by and large content to buy or build large suburban houses in place of country houses reflecting a desire and aspiration to be treated as a member of the urban societies not as part of the landed elite. Though country houses were still being constructed (**Hill of Tarvit**, 1906, **Formakin**, 1903–12, and **Blebo Craigs House**, 1910 [plate 91]) the tide had already turned, and the country house was in retreat.

The safe, secure, and organised world of Edwardian Britain crashed between 1914 and 1918. Just as servants were becoming difficult to engage the First, and then the Second World Wars altered British society and social outlook entirely. The forces of social change gathered pace as War acted as a focusing catalyst. In particular the position of women in the workplace was altered with far reaching consequences for society as a whole.

These changes were mirrored in the political life of the nation with the increased electoral support for the Labour Party and socialist policies. This shift in the electorate's political allegiances and expectations came at the expense of the Liberal Party, formerly the main reforming movement in the country. After WWII Labour successfully placed its message before the populace and won the first postwar election. The enthusiasm for a Labour government clearly indicated the desire of the people of a war-ravaged country for radical change, and for a better future than the recent past. It was not just the mood of the times, but a bench mark on the process of gradual social change which was affecting the whole nation.

Labour's egalitarian social policies aimed at ensuring equality of the individual through legislating fiscal measures to force the 'haves' and the wealthiest in society to contribute to improvements for the 'have nots', the poor and the disadvantaged. They introduced higher levels of taxation and death duties, bringing about a real fear in some quarters of some sort of land nationalisation. The country house owner faced the loss of positions of importance which many had taken generations to achieve. The country house was caught in a financial squeeze. In addition to the cost of servants' wages, all the other important expenses of running a country house merely compounded existing difficulties.

The country house became a financial burden from which many retreated with all haste. In 1884 Joseph Chamberlain commented that

> 'almost universally throughout England and Scotland agriculture
> has become a ruinous occupation'. [26]

Without the social and entertainment value of the house to the owner such properties were drains down which money poured with little hope of return. The first step in the attempts to retain position was the consolidation of estates, so that at least one viable country house might survive intact. For those owners of many properties the outlying, or infrequently used mansions were given over to other uses. Many

Plate 91
Blebo Craigs House, Fife.

became schools or hospitals, easily adaptable to institutional life. Only a few were given to the care of the National Trust for Scotland. Few Scottish landowners held more than one estate. In general Scottish owners were fighting for the survival of not only their principal seat, but also of their only residence.

If these measures did not succeed in securing the estate then a portion of the land could be sold off. Portions of the house itself could be closed off (as at Crawford Priory [plate 92, 93, 94]) to hopefully be reopened later. This usually staved off the destruction for no more than a few years, as, if attempts were made to reopen a closed wing, it was certain to be found in need of total restoration and renovation – only further expense. Another, more drastic option, only too common in Scotland was to exploit a legal loophole in the Local Authority rating

Plate 93 (opposite, above)
Crawford Priory, Fife.
The Georgian house
encased in Gothic dress.

Plate 94 (opposite, below)
Crawford Priory, Fife.
Extensive ecclesiastical
Gothic additions now in
ruins.

Plate 95
Largo House, Fife. The
ruinous entrance facade.

Plate 96
Strichen House, Grampian.
The entrance facade.
(RCAHMS)

Plate 97
Mavis Bank House, Lothian.

procedure by removing the roof of the property to exempt it from rates. This happened across Scotland (such as at Largo House [plate 95]). The results were often disastrous. In many cases it was as good as total demolition [plate 96].

Between 1946 and 1970 216 houses of architectural merit were lost. Uncharacteristically, in comparison with England, almost 50% of these losses occurred after 1960! Whilst in England many of the country houses had long established reputations and historical associations,

Scotland, it was paradoxically felt, offered few of these attractions. A certain academic snobbery was apparent in the downgrading of Scottish country houses in comparison with their English counterparts. Perhaps also the fact that the administration of Scotland's government systems was being directed from Westminster cannot have helped the situation either. The resultant ignorance about not only the dire state of the country houses of Scotland, but also their unique and excellent architectural heritage, rendered to rubble numerous properties.

How significantly ignorance of the real state of affairs in Scotland contributed to the destruction of country houses north of the border can only be guessed at. When combined with the financial and social changes which attacked these symbols of privilege there could be little surprise that even more estates had not succumbed to decay. [plate 97]

CHAPTER 9

The Survival of the Country House

*D*espite the continued loss of important country houses – recently half of **Minto House** [plate 98] has fallen prey to demolition, and **Mar Lodge** (built in 1896 for the Duke of Fife by Marshall MacKenzie) was virtually destroyed by fire during the closing stages of extensive renovation – some good news of restorations and renovations has been forthcoming. The question of how and if other country houses can be saved is a broad one. The problem with country houses is that they were designed to be the centre-piece for large working estates, or backed up by substantial financial reserves from profitable industrial ventures or from professional and political careers. In addition they reflected a particular method through which and by which the nation was governed. Most of these features are not securely fixed or permanent. Today the sands of time are constantly shifting.

What is surprising indeed, despite the impression to the contrary, is the number of country houses that have survived to the present day,

Plate 98
Minto House, Borders. Half the house has now indeed been demolished. (RCAHMS)

142

and that there are others which are being brought back to life. Some houses, the swan song designs of the Gothic Revival and Scottish Baronial architects, cannot be brought back in the same manner simply because almost as soon as they were built they became obsolete. **Kildonan House** [plate 99, 100] is a perfect example of this trait. One of the last houses in the Gothic tradition, it was built for Captain the Honourable Ewan Wallace, an MP from 1910–15. Wallace had inherited 30,000 acres of land upon which the house was to be built, from an uncle. The house was overly large and inadequately placed to meet the challenges of the twentieth century. In a similar vein was the vast Baronial pile of **Sauchieburn Castle** [plate 101] in Stirlingshire. The house was designed for Sir James Maitland, Bt by the architectural firm of Sydney Mitchell & Wilson. Nothing now remains of Sauchieburn Castle. The site of David Bryce's **Seacliffe House** [plate 102] is a tale of

Plate 99 (top)
Kildonan, Ayrshire, 1914. The garden facade, accented and articulated by dormers and sweeping roof lines.

Plate 100 (above)
Kildonan, Ayrshire, 1914. The entrance courtyard.

Plate 101
Sauchieburn Castle, Central,
1890.
(RCAHMS)

similar abandonment.

If houses could not adapt in the short term to change they could not then survive beyond, in many cases, the Second World War. Possibilities in resurrecting the fortunes of a country house do exist, and some successful examples of re-use and restoration shine out of the general mist and gloom. However the evidence is patchy and difficult to collate as no index of country houses in Scotland yet exists. Across the country as a whole properties are largely therefore unknown and

144

the definition of what, in the late twentieth century, constitutes a country house is problematic. Recently John Martin Robinson suggested that the country house had weathered and survived the worst vagaries of the storm, and that a future for country houses as the centre pieces of estates was possible and happening across the nation. But as he himself admitted

'Definition… does pose a problem in that there are a lot of architec-

145

Plate 102
Seacliffe House, East
Lothian.
(RCAHMS. By Neil
Jackson, Bryce Exhibition
Committee.)

*turally interesting new houses which are not the centres of estates
when some which are, especially in Scotland, are little better than
bungalows'.* [27]

In tandem with the rebirth of the Scottish Country House has been the
various restorations of decayed estates and tower houses – these do not
strictly fit the image of the country house proper, but they signpost the
romantic yearning of some individuals to recreate the past. This is in
the main through the use of Scottish classicism and vernacular precedent. For example **Monteviot House** and **Aboyne Castle** fit into this
category. Monteviot was remodelled for the Marquis of Midlothian.
The core of the house, and eighteenth century building, was retained
whilst Tudor-Gothic additions by the Victorian architect Blore were
reconstructed and internally remodelled. A new front of neo-Georgian
classicism was added with white harling and carved heraldic panels.
Aboyne was given a similar remodelling through the rationalisation of
the plan and the reharling of the exterior of the new, smaller mansion.

To some extent these country houses reflect the contraction – in both
physical and philosophical terms – of the position of the country
houses. This is especially true on a simple level in that they are on a
more domestic and intimately human scale than their strident and
forceful Victorian counterparts. In addition they invariably involve the
rebuilding of existing structures which in turn involves a reduction in
the physical size of the house. In a sense these mansions are a return to
the values espoused by the styles they seek to imitate – simplicity and
utility. The country house has contracted to fulfil a reduced version and

vision of its traditional role of importance in local life. Perhaps this mirrors the way in which the estates themselves have also contracted. Their motto has been both simple and effective – 'adapt or die'.

The fortunes of the country house undoubtedly fell during the Second World War and its aftermath – country houses were requisitioned for the War effort and used as hospitals, schools, store houses, or, often with dire consequences, army barracks or army headquarters. In addition war-time regulations aimed at conserving scarce national resources at a time of emergency hung over the first decade of the peace-time years. Building works and the constant demands of the upkeep of a country house were almost completely suspended for the duration under the 1941 Building Licence, Defence Regulations. These were only abolished in 1954 – little wonder therefore that many country houses fell into disrepair.

The fears and suspicions of the 1945 Labour Government by the landed classes and country house owners were deeply felt in some quarters. Change was real, wide ranging, and apparently on the increase – the introduction of the welfare state, nationalisation, the introduction of broader access to university education, and the rapid growth of the suburban middle classes. These developments all placed a strain on society which some believed would remove country houses entirely from the map of the nation. There was an undoubted retrenchment – for example the Gilmour family, which had given Scotland its first modern Secretary of State for Scotland, gave up **Montrave House** [plate 103] to demolition by explosion as late as 1971. What they did not forsake was their estate. They adapted to circumstances and, just as at Penicuik House, after the fire of 1899, the stable block was adapted to new purposes to serve as a country house.

What are the reasons then for the survival of the country house in Scotland? They are in many ways complex and confused. Firstly, Scotland had a traditional image of sporting estates – the Balmoral image, so to speak. Scotland also had a social season – running from August through to the New Year, from grouse shoots to Highland Christmas parties and Highland 'Caledonian' society balls in Edinburgh, and the Islands at Hogmanay. Scottish country houses

Plate 103
Montrave House, Fife.
View of the house c.1899.

Plate 104
Dupplin Castle, Tayside, 1828.

could offer something unique – they could offer the romance and the image of tourist Scotland.

Secondly, though Scottish country houses did fall drastically in numbers many owners were determined to retain a country seat at the centre of a landed estate. There was a committed resilience in the struggle to retain a fully functioning country house, of whatever size as the focal point of the estate.

Thirdly, those estate owners who had survived the worst ravages of the decades of the twentieth century with their property more or less intact were able to take advantage of the leaps in domestic technology occurring after the 1960s. From central heating to varied domestic appliances, to security systems and all the labour saving devices for the kitchens. Servants became much less of a necessity, and each of these advances gradually made life without servants much easier. The house

Plate 105
Dupplin Castle, Tayside, 1970.

would no longer need to incur such high labour costs.

Those country houses best suited to survival as mansions at the centre of estates were small houses, based on the wealth generated by the land itself. Large country houses were of little useful purpose, and country houses with extensive servants quarters fared the worst of all. In the 1930s, for example, when William Burn's **Dupplin Castle** [plate 104] burnt down it was not rebuilt, but remained a mutilated shell of its former self. Only in 1970 did Lord Teviot build a severely classical Scottish mansion [plate 105] on the same site. The spectacular outlook of the property – on the very ridge of a steep hill – was used to its fullest extent through the marriage of a reinforced concrete raft (for the new foundations) and the remaining substructure of the dramatic Burn mansion.

Country houses also found new uses – such as Oxenfoord Castle becoming a school (though this school itself recently closed). Many country houses were found new leases of life partitioned into apartments and flats. Examples can be seen in the successful **Tyninghame**, and **Kilmany**, to **Poltallach House** [plate 106]. The recent history of the last mansion – Poltalloch House – is however yet another object lesson in the changeable fortunes facing country houses. In the 1950s this William Burn house was split into flats. These remained occupied until 1970 when moves were made to sell the house as one lot. Buyers could not be found for such an isolated, though hauntingly beautiful mansion, and the property fell into disrepair and ruin. Other houses became hotels, holiday homes, or conference facilities. Country house re-use as hotels has proved a popular choice – though not always with

Plate 106
Poltalloch House, Argyll, 1850.
View of the ruins of Poltalloch, with the ruins of the conservatory to the left of the picture.

Plate 107
House of Gray, Tayside,
1715.

success, and something of questionable judgement in some instances. The reasons for the popularity are simple – country house hotels at the very best end of the market provide both the luxury and grand style of a formal country house, whilst at the same time providing the intimacy and the domesticity of a 'private' house. Country house hotels are marketed as places of holiday and relaxation, somewhere uniquely offering both the touch of the past and all the benefits of the modern world.

Other country houses have courted survival by becoming part of Scotland's biggest single industry – becoming part of the tourist industry. Those who have done so successfully are true exemplars of country house adaptation and survival. After all the country house is a business which its owner has, by definition, to exploit to its fullest potential. Floors Castle, Hopetoun House, Mellerstain, Manderstoun, Dalmeny. These are all in private hands – as distinct from the works of the National Trust for Scotland – and they manage their best to thrive in a very competitive market place. Still others sought shelter from the ravages of change within the comforts of the National Trust for Scotland – houses such as Culzean, Haddo House, House of Dun, or Hill of Tarvit. Finally others still have retained their independence by establishing heritable trusts to ensure the survival of the mansion and of the estate within the hands of the family, allowing it to pass from generation to generation. But, of course this does not exclude the possibility of the twists of fate that may lie in wait.

To what use then can isolated buildings in the country be put? That is the real question that has to be asked of anyone attempting to resurrect the shells of ruined mansions for new uses. Some country houses are undoubtedly fortunate in that they are close to growing urban sprawls and can be used as part of commercial or cultural developments. Two examples of this type of rescue are the **House of Gray** [plate 107, figure 47], by Dundee, and **Chatelherault** at Hamilton. The House of Gray is currently being transformed from a shell into a hotel and conference centre. Part of the conditions for grant aid is the restoration of the main public rooms in the William Adam manner.

Chatelherault [plate 108] was originally completed by William Adam in 1754 as a banqueting hall and dog kennels, and also the terminal feature on the main tree avenue, cutting a swathe amongst some 10,000 trees planted on the Duke's orders from 1703–32, between Hamilton Palace and the edge of their estate leading up to their old family seat the castle of Cadzow. In 1944 the banqueting hall was destroyed by fire, and almost all of William Adam's exquisite plasterwork designs were lost. Until 1978 the building stood forlorn and rejected on the edge of the estate. Then, as part of death duties the government acquired some 350 acres and the building. Over the years up to 1988 some £4 million was spent on the stabilisation of the building and the recreation of its original eighteenth century splen-

Figure 47
House of Gray, Dundee, Tayside.
Ground floor plan to designs of William Adam.

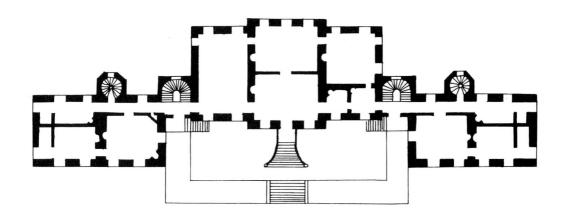

Plate 108
Chatelherault, Strathclyde,
1731.

Plate 109 (opposite)
Crawford Priory, Fife – the
main entrance.

dour. The restorers were fortunate in that the building had been photographed by *Country Life* magazine in 1919, prior to the demolition of Hamilton Palace; it was from these photographs and painful archeological research that the restoration of Chatelherault was possible.

The **House of Dun** has also been rescued from twentieth-century expedients and restored by the National Trust for Scotland. The house was used as a hunting, shooting, and fishing estate and hotel until recently. When the building entered the care of the Trust a decision was made to restore the house as far as possible to its original concept, whilst at the same time ensuring that the rooms in the house would be entertaining and open to interesting interpretation. The house was reopened to the public in 1989.

What is strange about these three restorations is that each building was designed by or has a connection with the work of the architect William Adam. Indeed the major restoration that is currently underway at **Duff House** to turn that property into one of the new 'remote' galleries for the National Museums of Scotland also concerns a building by Adam. There are other architects and buildings crying out for immediate attention and support. William Adam, whilst acknowledged as one of Scotland's most important architects, should not dominate the field or the resources. Other properties need conservation – but to be realistic they firstly need a useful new life. More often than not today that useful life is perceived as being one of public use and not for private family enjoyment. That is the challenge of the restorer. If these houses cease to be houses and homes, what else can they become without alienating their character and traditions? [plate 109]

Gazetteer

Many of the Country Houses described in this book are open to the public, or are visible from a public road or nearby footpath. Many are also private homes, and readers are requested to respect the privacy of the owners and occupiers of these buildings. Not all of Scotland's greatest country houses are mentioned here, merely some of the most interesting, those connected with this book, and those which may be of interest to the reader.

A: Architect   C: Client

Abbotsford House, Melrose, Borders.
A William Atkinson; C Sir Walter Scott. 1816.
Tudor and Scots-Jacobean manor-house, a proto-Scottish-Baronial mansion of great significance.

Aden House, Old Deer, Banff and Buchan, Grampian.
A John Smith; C Russell of Moncoffer family. 1832.
Additions to 1750 mansion, Greek Doric order, entrance front with porte-cochere, bow projection through two storeys to garden front. Now a ruin.

Aboyne Castle, Aboyne, Grampian.
A John Lamb; C Lord Aboyne. 1983.
Remodelling and reduction of Victorianised castle, reinstatement of harling.

Airthrey Castle, Stirling, Central.
A Robert and James Adam; C Robert Haldane. 1790.
'D' shaped Adam castle with a great variety of oddly-shaped rooms. Now part of Stirling University, with unsympathetic additions.

Amisfield House, Haddington, East Lothian.
A Isaac Ware; C Francis Charteris. 1755.
Most important building in the orthodox Palladian school; seven bays, central Ionic portico. Demolished 1928.

Arbigland House, Dumfries, Dumfries & Galloway.
A William Craik; C William Craik. 1755.
One room deep, five bays wide (with the central three articulated by Ionic pilasters and pedimented), and with connecting single storey pavilions Arbigland was created by Craik for himself in 1755.

Archerfield House, Dirleton, East Lothian.
A Unknown; C Sir John Nisbet. 1633.
A John Douglas; C William Nisbet. 1730.
A Robert Adam; C William Nisbet of Dirleton. 1789.
Extensive alterations and additions to late C17th house, unusual bow projection entrance front (matched by similar to garden side), entrance courtyard with quadrant links. 1962 interiors removed, building given over to grain store.

Ardkinglas, Cairndow, Argyll.
A Sir Robert Lorimer; C Sir Andrew Noble, Bt. 1906.
New Baronial mansion with terraces and gardens and own hydro-electric powerhouse. Variety of roof levels and crow stepped gables. Intended harling not executed.

Ardmaddy Castle, Seil Sound, Argyll.
A Unknown; C Campbell family. 1737.
Two storey house with its back firmly against the sea, in a dramatic landscape overlooking a

secluded walled garden. The pedimented centre sits atop a deep recess, the Ionic order used in a naive Palladian interpretation.

Arniston House, Gorebridge, Midlothian.
A William Adam; C Robert Dundas. 1726.
Nine bay (N) entrance front with a three bay recessed centre; attached Ionic columns and heraldic pediment.

Auchinleck House, Ochiltree, Strathclyde.
A John Adam; C Alexander Boswell, Lord Auchinleck. 1754.
Five bay by three house, with Ionic pilastered three bay advanced central feature. Closely related in style and treatment to the nearby Dumfries House.

Balbirnie House, Glenrothes, Fife.
A Richard Crichton; C General Robert Balfour. 1815
Eleven Bay house with Ionic portico entrance. Crisp detailing and clean, clear lines – a Neo-classical house of some elegance. Now an hotel.

Balcarres, Colinsburgh, Fife.
A William Burn; C Robert Lindsay. 1834.
A William Burn; C James Lindsay. 1838
A David Bryce; C Sir Coutts Lindsay. 1863.
Three generations of same family involved in the extensive remodelling of the same property. Originally a sixteenth century laird's house, curiously unsatisfying mixture of Elizabethan and Baronial. Sir Robert Lorimer provided gatelodges for the estate in 1896 for the Earl of Crawford and Balcarres.

Balcaskie, St Monans, Fife.
A Sir William Bruce; C Sir William Bruce. 1668.
Originally seventeeth century 'L' shaped house built for Moncrieffs of Balcaskie. Terraced garden created to south, plan regularised, quadrant links added 1670/2. Burn and Bryce alterations in 1830 and 1856 respectively.

Balloch Castle, Balloch, Strathclyde.

A Robert Lugar; C John Buchan of Ardoch. 1809.
Castle-gothic house, influenced by Inverary Castle and the nearby (now demolished) Tullichewan Castle. Asymmetrical floor plan and irregular skyline combine to picturesque effect.

Ballochmyle House, Catrine, Strathclyde.
A John Adam; C Allan Whitefoord. 1757.
Chaste house, extensively remodelled 1886 in both Georgian and Jacobean detailing by Hew Montgomerie Wardrop. Now vacant and in need of restoration.

Balmano Castle, Glenfarg, Perthshire.
A Sir Robert Lorimer; C S.W. Miller. 1916.
Remodelling earlier seventeenth century castle in Lorimer's Arts & Crafts Baronial style. Extensive garden works.

Balmoral Castle, Crathie, Grampian.
A William Smith; C Queen Victoria and Prince Albert. 1855.
Scottish Baronial at its most Germanic, dominated by a surging tower and over muscular porte-cochere. Exterior visibly demonstrates the social functions of the house and the distinctions between levels in Victorian society.

Balvenie House, Dufftown, Grampian.
A James Gibbs; C William Duff of Braco. 1724.
Modest mansion in plain classical style, square tripartite plan, two storeys over rustic, seven bay facade (central three pedimented and advanced). Became part of a distillery, demolished 1929.

Banff Castle, Banff, Grampian.
A John Adam; C Lord Deskford. 1750.
Five bay facade, harled with stone dressings. Perhaps intended to possess a small pediment above the central bay, given the articulation of the fenestration. Prominent site overlooking Banff.

Barbreck House, Barbreck, Argyll.

1790 classic harled mansion with five bay main house (central three bays slightly advanced) matching linked bays of single storey with venetian windows.

Birkhill, Fife.
A David Bryce. 1857.
Scottish Baronial mansion, reconstructed out of an earlier house. For romantic effect in a romantic setting.

Blairquharran Castle, Straiton, Strathclyde.
A William Burn; C Sir David Hunter. 1820.
Tudor-Gothic much in the manner of William Wilkins and Inverary Castle. Dominated by the central lantern tower and porte-cochere, introduction of gables, elements treated in a symmetrical manner.

Blebo Craigs House, Kemback, Fife.
Almost hidden delight of a country house, solid classical nineteenth century with additions in 1903 by James Findlay – round tower and dormer windows. Secluded setting.

Blythswood House, Glasgow, Strathclyde.
A James Playfair; C Archibald Campbell. 1787.
Enlargement of existing house to form a nine bay main block (central three bays advanced with Doric porte-corchere) and adjoining three storey three bay service blocks. Demolished 1928.

Bow Hill, Selkirk, Borders.
A William Atkinson; C Duke of Buccleuch. 1812.
Additions to eighteenth century house. Became favourite family seat in preference over Dalkeith Palace. Later additions by William Burn and David Bryce creating one long classical facade.

Broomhall, Limelinks, Fife.
A Thomas Harrison; C 5th Earl of Elgin and 9th earl of Kincardine. 1796.
Eleven bay house with delightful bow projection on the garden front. Two storeys above a rustic, with restrained Ionic Order on the bow.

Cairness House, Buchan, Grampian.
A James Playfair; C Charles Gordon. 1791.
Two storeys above a half sunk rustic, five bays wide with two end bays in a restrained Doric and French Neo-Classical style with some Egyptian motifs thrown in.

Caldwell Castle, Uplawmoor, Strathclyde.
A Robert Adam; C Baron William Mure. 1771.
Three storey Adam symmetrical castle with castellated skyline above triumphal arch motifs, bartizans and conical pepper-pots on each of the four turrets articulating the five bay facade.

Cambo House, Kingsbarns, Fife.
A Wardrop & Reid; C Sir Thomas Erskine of Cambo. 1879.
Large Italianate Georgian villa in red sandstone built to replace an earlier mansion destroyed by fire (the family rallied round to furnish the new house). 1884 additions included a clock tower.

Cambusnethan Priory, Wishaw, Strathclyde.
A James Gillespie Graham; C Robert Lockhart. 1816.
Large Gothic house in a monastic style, not wholly successful, though arguably perhaps the best example of the architect's work. Here his usual trademark of a round tower dominating the composition was replaced by an octagonal tower. The house is now derelict and a victim of vandalism.

Camperdown House, Dundee, Tayside.
A William Burn; C Lord Camperdown. 1824.
Simplified Ionic mansion resting in a perfectly suited landscape. Portico entrance with fine views across the south and west. Burn's knack of planning successfully hid the servants' quarters from view.

Carstairs House, Carstairs, Strathclyde.
A William Burn; C Henry Monteith. 1822.
Tudor-Gothic mansion on a raised site, distinctive scrolled gables (some merely deco-

rative) dominated by the lantern tower.

Charleton House, Colinsburgh, Fife.
A John Adam; C John Thompson of Charleton. 1749.
With purchase of Newton Estate in 1740 John Thompson built a new house and changed name of estate to Charleton. Classical Villa with later additions by William Burn and Robert Lorimer.

Chatelherault, Fernigair, Hamilton, Strathclyde.
A William Adam; C 5th Duke of Hamilton. 1731.
Hunting lodge and eye-catcher built to provide a terminal point to the formal landscape at Hamilton Palace, and to fulfil the Duke's boast. Extensively damaged by fire and mine workings, now restored.

Craighall, Ceres, Fife.
A Sir William Bruce; C Sir William Hope. 1679.
Extensive remodelling and regularising of an earlier building into a significant classical mansion house. The most unusual feature was a semi-circular pediment which ran over three bays. The house was demolished in 1955.

Craigiehall House, Edinburgh, Lothian.
A Sir William Bruce; C Lord Annandale. 1694.
Two storeys over half sunk rustic, six bay facade (central two slightly advanced with heraldic pediment) on a tripartite plan.

Crawford Priory, Cults, Fife.
A David Hamilton; C Lady Mary Lindsay. 1810.
A James Gillespie Graham; C Lady Mary Lindsay. 1810.
Perhaps the most important Gothic Priory house in Scotland, recasting of an earlier eighteenth centuryhouse in ecclesiastical dress. Derelict since 1971 and in need of restoration.

Culdees Castle, Tayside.
A James Gillespie Graham; C General Andrew John Drummond. 1810.
Castellation mansion where the influence of

Inverary Castle is once again apparent. The entrance front has three square towers, and is dominated by the three storey drum tower rising at the back of the house.

Culzean Castle, Maybole, Strathclyde.
A Robert Adam; C 10th Earl of Cassilis. 1777.
Most imposing of Adam's castle style buildings, with a dramatic and romantic cliff top position. The main body of Adam's design remains within his classical and symmetrical tradition, and it is only the seaward side which is irregularly planned – and that only at the close of Adam's career.

Dalkieth Palace, Dalkieth, Midlothian.
A James Smith; C Duchess of Buccleuch. 1702.
Creation of regular plan and facade. Three storey blocks step up to four toward the centre, with an engaged portico of fluted Corinthian pilasters.

Dalmeny House, South Queensferry, West Lothian.
A William Wilkins; C 4th Earl of Roseberry. 1815.
Introduced the Gothic Revival into Scotland's country houses, though underlying formality of plan still evidenced on the exterior. Elizabethan dress clothing the segmented apartments of public, private and servant rooms.

Dalquharran Castle, Dailly, Strathclyde.
A Robert Adam; C Thomas Kennedy. 1782.
Perhaps the finest of Robert Adam's classical castles, with imposing and clear detailing built for Adam's niece. The house is dominated by a round bastion tower, looking out across the surrounding landscape. Extended in the 1880s by Wardrop & Reid the house during twentieth century fell into disuse and is now derelict.

Douglas Castle, Douglas, Strathclyde.
A John and James Adam; C 1st Duke of Douglas. 1757.
Direct descendant of Inverary Castle. Only

half of the Adam castle was ever built in its classical neo-Gothic style. The castle was demolished in 1951.

Donibristle House, Aberdour, Fife.
A James Smith & Alexander McGill; C 5th & 6th Earls of Moray. 1719.
Piend roofed extended mansion with matching harled pavilions. Fire damaged the central portion in 1858, and the two pavilions have remained unconnected since then.

Drumlanrig Castle, Thornhill, Dumfries & Galloway.
A James Smith; C Duke of Buccleuch. 1679.
Imposing red sandstone mansion set in formal landscape, a curious mixture of classical arcades, pilasters, and pediments integrated into an almost defensive castle-like building.

Duddingston House, Edinburgh, Midlothian.
A Sir William Chambers; C 8th Earl of Abercorn. 1762.
A classical 'Grecian' villa of five bays dominated by a composite order and pedimented portico over the central three bays. Symmetrically planned offices and kitchen court set off asymmetrically to the main house.

Duff House, Banff, Grampian.
A William Adam; C Lord Braco. 1735.
As built a nine bay house, with a pediment slightly advanced from the attic storey over the central three bays. Corner towers articulated the plan, and held service stairwells. Some of William Adam's most crisp detailing, though a mansion never realised in its intended conception. Virtually unused by the family the house passed into local government care in the early C20th. Now being renovated as an out-post gallery.

Dumfries House, Cumnock, Strathclyde.
A Robert Adam; C 4th Earl of Dumfries. 1754.
Nine bay house with linked quadrant pavilions, central three bays slightly advanced with a heraldic pediment; two storeys over a half sunk rustic. Later additions have not affected the restrained classical simplicity of the facades.

Dun (House of), Montrose, Tayside.
A William Adam; C John Erskine, later Lord Erskine. 1730.
Entrance facade dominated by the triumphal arch motif which rises the full height of the mansion. The garden front is no less exuberant, yet is somehow also restrained – perhaps because the house did not become the centre of the grandiose formal gardens planned by the Earl of Mar. The house has recently been painstakingly restored by the NTS.

Dunalistair House, Kinloch Rannoch, Tayside.
A Andrew Heiton & Son; C General Sir John MacDonald. 1852.
Scottish Baronial mansion with a Francophile swagger, crow stepped gables and pepperpot towers. Now derelict.

Dundas Castle, South Queensferry, Midlothian.
A William Burn; C James Dundas. 1818.
Rebuilt by Burn in a castellated plain Tudor-Gothic style, a functional country house.

Dundeave Castle, Inverary, Argyll.
A Sir Robert Lorimer; C Sir Andrew Noble. 1911.
Restoration and additions to a sixteenth century castle in Lorimer's Scottish Arts & Crafts Vernacular style.

Dunkeld House, Dunkeld, Tayside.
A William Bruce; C Marquess of Atholl. 1676.
Seven by five bay house, built on tripartite plan, given a harled finish. Demolished in 1830 in preparation for a much larger house which never materialised.

Dunmore Park, Airth, Central.
A William Wilkins; C 5th Earl of Dunmore. 1820.
Wilkins' second Elizabethan Tudor country house in Scotland and directly comparable to the earlier Dalmeny House. The entrance front

dominated by a large porte-corchere. Now derelict.

Dunninald House, Graig, Angus, Tayside.
A James Gillespie Graham; C Peter Arkly. 1823.
Typical Gillespie Graham castle style mansion, the composition of the main house of six bays offset by a three storey building round tower rising above the house. Window openings self consciously 'Norman', 'Gothic' and 'Georgian Gothick'. The all pervasive influence of Inverary Castle remains, as does the contemporary influence of Robert Lugar.

Duntrune House, Burnside of Duntrune, Dundee, Tayside.
A William burn; C William Stirling Graham. 1824.
Tudor Gothic mansion house, at the centre of a working estate. Workmanlike execution.

Dunrobin Castle, Golspie, Highland.
A Charles Barry; C 2nd Duke of Sutherland. 1850.
Extensive remodelling of existing structure to create possibly the most extravagant chateau castle, and very Bavarian in its impression. The Victorian additions tripled the size of the house, dwarfing the original castle into insignificance.

Dupplin Castle, Aberdalgie, Tayside.
A James Smith. 1688.
A William Burn; C 10th Earl of Kintoul. 1828.
A Schomberg Scott; C Lord Teviot. 1970.
The first house was a classical mansion destroyed by fire in 1827. The Burn replacement was extravagantly Jacobean, and made excellent use of a difficult site. This mansion was demolished in 1967 to be replaced with a Scottish Vernacular classical house of white harling and stone dressings.

Earlshall Castle, Leuchars, Fife.
A Sir Robert Lorimer; C Robert W.R. MacKenzie. 1895.
Lorimer's first major commission involving the renovation of a tower house dating from 1546. A gatehouse was added in 1900. The most imposing feature is the spectacular gardens, designed by Lorimer.

Edmonstone Castle, Biggar, Lanark, Strathclyde.
A James Gillespie Graham; C James Brown. 1815.
Castle style mansion in a suitably romantic setting.

Eglinton Castle, Eglinton, Ayrshire.
A John Paterson; C Hugh Montgomerie, 12th Earl of Eglington. 1797.
Large castellated mansion much in the Adam castle style quadrangular in plan with round towers on each corner and a bow projection above the arched entrance. The house was unroofed in 1925, and virtually demolished through use as target practice on a gunnery range.

Falkland (House of), Falkland, Fife.
A William Burn; C O. Tyndall-Bruce. 1839.
Large Tudor Jacobean mansion, one of Burn's best country houses, with a wealth of exterior detailing consisting of crow stepped gables and square turreting.

Fasque House, Fasque, Grampian.
A John Paterson; C Sir Alexander Ramsay Bt. 1809.
Austere two storey house dominated by a central polygonal tower. Built of red sandstone and devoid of decoration.

Fettercairn Castle, Laurencekirk, Grampian.
A William Burn; C Sir William Forbes. 1826.
Burn reconstructed an earlier mansion with Jacobean-Gothic clothes, raising the main rooms to the piano nobile and counter balancing the horizontal emphasis of the design through the use of curved gables above almost every window.

Floors Castle, Kelso, Borders.
A William Adam; C 1st Duke of Roxburgh. 1721.

The first major commission for Adam. and one in essence unsatisfactory in execution, none of the features (axial planning, connected and ranked suites of rooms etc) were present. The house was remodelled by David Bryce in the mid nineteenth century.

Formakin, Bishopton, Renfrew, Strathclyde.
A Sir Robert Lorimer; C John A. Holms. 1908.
Creation of Scots Baronial mansion within a formal landscape, drawing on Lorimer's favourite fifteenth and sixteenth century motifs. The house was to surround Holms' fine art collection. Uncompleted the house sits in the midst of a country park.

Gosford House, Longniddry, East Lothian.
A Robert Adam; C 7th Earl of Wemyss. 1790.
Largest of Robert Adam's classical mansions, designed to house a famous art collection. The Adam house was never fully realised and the wings either side of the central block were replaced in 1890 (one since gutted by fire).

Gray (House of), Denhead of Gray, Tayside.
A William Adam; C 10th Lord Gray. 1715.
Classical Scottish-Palladian villa with two storey pavilions attached to the main house by octagonal staircase towers. The three central bays are topped by a heraldic pediment. The house is currently undergoing major restoration after total dereliction.

Haddo House, Methlick, Grampian.
A William Adam; C 2nd Earl of Aberdeen. 1732.
Classical villa house of three storeys, seven bay facade with central three pedimented. Two office pavilions with quadrant links. Now in the care of the NTS.

Hall Teases, Ceres, Fife.
A William Burn; C Robert Christie. 1825.
Jacobean mansion dominated by a central tower.

Hamilton Palace, Hamilton, Strathclyde.
A James Smith; C 3rd Duke and Duchess of Hamilton. 1693.
Rebuilding of Hamilton Palace in a muscular Corinthian order, the house was added to by William Adam (1717) and David Hamilton (1822). The whole edifice was demolished in 1920.

Hill of Tarvit, Ceres, Fife.
A Sir Robert Lorimer; C Frederick B. Sharp. 1906.
Large alterations involving the demolition of a Bruce attributed mansion (Wemysshall) to create a Lorimer house in the Scottish Vernacular Free Style. Harled with stone dressings, loggia entrance courtyard, garden facade to south with symmetrical bow wing projections across terracing. Built to house and surround an impressive private art collection. Property of NTS.

Hopetoun House, South Queensferry, East Lothian.
A Sir William Bruce; C Charles Hope. 1699.
A William Adam; C 1st & 2nd Earls of Hopetoun. 1723.
A Robert Adam; C 2nd Earl of Hopetoun. 1750.
Creation of the finest classical house in Scotland, an imposing house with quadrant links to massive pavilions, originally set within extensive formal gardens.

Inverary Castle, Inverary, Argyll.
A Rodger Morris; C 3rd Duke of Argyll. 1744.
The signpost country house in the development of the gothic and castle style mansions. Influenced by Sir John Vanburgh's designs supplied to the Dukes of Argyll and the Campbell family's desire to maintain their native Scottishness. Essentially a classical building in castellated and gothic dress.

Jerviston House, Holytown, Monklands, Strathclyde.
A Robert and James Adam; C James Cannison. 1782.
Elegant mansion of three storeys by three bays, triumphal arch motif, a venetian

window with two Doric pilasters rising to support a pediment above one bay all unite in a balanced composition; given horizontal emphasis by the two single storey pavilions.

Keil House, Southend, Argyll.
A Campbell, Douglas & Sellars; C J.N. Fleming. 1870.
Vigorous English vernacular revival style, much in the manner of Richard Norman Shaw with sweeping roofs and a dominant tower. Became a school. Suffered fire damage and now derelict.

Kellie Castle, Pittenweem, Fife.
A Not recorded; C Erskine family. 1603.
A fine example of a Scottish Renaissance chateau. The summer home of the Lorimer family from the 1870s. Now in the care of the NTS.

Kennet House, Kennet, Central.
A Thomas Harrison; C Bruce of Kennet. 1795.
On the entrance front a two storey neo-classical building, with the sunk basement the garden front showed the house to be three storeys. Semi-circular porch and tripartite windows. Demolished 1967.

Kildonan, Barrhill, Strathclyde.
A James Miller; C Euan Wallace MP. 1914.
Large mansion in the English Tudor Manorial Revival style with broad sweeping roofs punctuated by several chimney stacks, dormers and gables. The house was never fully completed internally.

Kilconquhar Castle, Kilconquhar, Fife.
A William Burn; C Sir Henry Bethune Bt. 1831.
Additions and alterations in a Jacobean Scots Tudor style.

Kinfauns Castle, Kinfauns, Tayside.
A Sir Robert Smirke; C 15th Lord Gray. 1820.
Pink sandstone castellated mansion overlooking the Tay. The composition is a grouping of distinct symmetrical elements.

Kinnaird Castle, Kinnaird, Angus, Tayside.
A James Playfair; C Sir David Carnegie Bt. 1785.
Castellated mansion, largely remodelled and extended by David Bryce 1855. The house was badly damaged by fire in 1921.

Kinross House, Kinross, Tayside.
A Sir William Bruce; C Sir William Bruce. 1686.
Imposing four storey classical mansion in the tradition, linked quadrants, within formal geometrical garden setting. Rhythm of facade three bay five bay three bay, with central five bays slightly recessed.

Kirkdale House, Carsluth, Dumfries & Galloway.
A Robert Adam; C Sir Samuel Hannay. 1787.
Simple exterior (Adam's plans were scaled down) two main storeys over a rustic with an attic storey squeezed in atop. Two pavilions linked by straight corridors to the main house. The pavilions have tripartite windows and the north front of the house has a polygonal bay in the centre of the mansion.

Langside, Glasgow, Strathclyde.
A Robert Adam; C Thomas Brown. 1777.
Now demolished but significant in that it was one of the few Adam houses to link service courts to the main house with quadrant corridors.

Leslie House, Markinch, Fife.
A John Mylne; C John Leslie 7th Earl/1st Duke of Rothes. 1667.
First classical country house in Scotland, pedimented east front, courtyard plan with gallery on piano nobile. Partially destroyed by fire 1763.

Letterfourie, Buckie, Grampian.
A Robert Adam; C James Gordon. 1773.
Three storeys over the basement level, three bays wide, with pavilions each of three bays – full of restrained classical dignity.

Manderston, Duns, Berwickshire, Borders.

A Alexander Gilkie/John White; C Dalhousie Weatherstone. 1790.
A James Simpson; C Sir William Miller. 1871.
A John Kinross; C Sir James Miller. 1890.
The house as it stands today is the work of Kinross. A classical house with the elegance of an eighteenth century Adam mansion. The main house has an Ionic portico and is eleven bays wide. Set in magnificent gardens.

Mellerstain Castle, Gordon, Borders.
A Robert Adam; C Hon George Baillie. 1770.
Adam provided the house with the main central block, after his father had apparently designed the servant wings in 1725. The house is one room in depth with the whole scheme united by a linking corridor running through the various units within the mansion. Impressive in the simplicity of its execution.

Melville House, Letham, Fife.
A James Smith; C 1st Earl of Melville. 1697.
Classical mansion approached via a formal tree lined avenue and an entrance forecourt with two quadrant pavilions. A squat 'H' plan with four storeys, a house of nine bays by six.

Melsetter House, Hoy, Orkney.
A William R. Lethaby; C Thomas Middlemore. 1898.
Remodelling of an existing laird's house to form an important Scottish Vernacular Arts & Crafts style mansion. Important because it was really the first to adopt this style in Scotland – despite being designed by an English architect for his English client. Also within the Scottish Baronial tradition.

Milton Lockhart, Carluke, Strathclyde.
A William Burn; C William Lockhart. 1829.
Robust Scots Vernacular style, developed by Burn out of the Tudor and Jacobean styles. Now demolished and sold for reconstruction to Japan.

Minto House, Hassendean, Borders.
A William Adam (Att); C Elliot family. 1738.
A Archibald Elliot; C Sir Gilbert Elliot, 1st Earl of Minto. 1809.
With the remodelling of a smaller existing mansion by William Adam an unusual 'V' shaped house was created. Archibald Elliot remodelled the house in a neo-classical style, adding the drum stairwell, dome lantern, and the Ionic semi-circular portico entrance. Not lived in as a house since WWII the mansion was partially demolished in 1993.

Moncrieffe House, Perth, Tayside.
A William Bruce; C Thomas Moncrieffe of that Ilk. 1676.
Compact tripartite square plan, seven bay entrance facade with broken pedimented entrance doorway, house was five bays deep. Demolished after fire destroyed house 1957.

Montrave House, Montrave, Fife.
A ; C John Gilmour. 1893.
Existing house, built by Major Alexander Anderson, was substantially redesigned in a grand Scottish Jacobean style. Demolished c.1970.

Monzie Castle, Monzie, Tayside.
A John Paterson; C General Campbell. 1795.
Adam-style castle almost devoid of decoration, relies on massing for effect. String courses mark off basement from piano nobile. Reconstructed by Lorimer after fire in 1908 (who provided furniture throughout the house).

Mount Melville, St Andrews, Fife.
A Paul Waterhouse; C James Younger. 1908.
Grand pink sandstone in a 'free style' with Baronial and Arts & Crafts overtones.

Newhailes House, Musselburgh, Midlothian.
A James Smith; C James Smith. 1690.
Originally called Whitehill James Smith built this unassuming classical mansion for himself. He designed a seven by three bay house of two storeys over a half sunk basement. The house was remodelled in the nineteenth century.

Newliston House, Newbridge, Lothian.

A Robert Adam; C Thomas Hogg. 1789.
A five bay entrance facade similar to the earlier Jerviston House – a pedimented centrepiece is here supported by Corinthian columns and nor Doric pilasters as at Jerviston. The latter are however used to decorate the bow projection at the rear of Newliston. The house is three storeys over a half sunk basement.

Ormiston House, Kirknewton, Midlothian.
A David Bryce; C Sir Alexander Wilkie. 1851.
Large Scottish Baronial mansion with crow stepped gables, corner towers and pepper pot turrets.

Overankeliour House, Bow of Fife, Fife.
Classical mansion of restrained elegance, nine bays, pedimented centre three, Ionic pilasters.

Oxenfoord Castle, Pathead, Lothian.
A Robert Adam; C Sir John Dalrymple Bt. 1780.
Adam castle, two floors above basement with round turrets flanking central portion. A carved horse and ox sit above the parapet on the east front. Latterly a girls' boarding school that is today no more.

Penicuik House, Penicuik, Midlothian.
A Sir John Clerk; C Sir John Clerk. 1760.
New classical mansion of thirteen bays, pedimented Ionic portico (with six columns) at centre three bays and end bays advanced with venetian windows. The house was severely damaged by fire in 1899.

Pitlour House, Strathmiglo, Fife.
A Robert Mylne; C General Philip Skene. 1775.
Modest, pared down classical mansion of five bays by two and two storeys over a rustic. The central three bays of the entrance facade are slightly advanced with a pediment atop.

Pollock House, Glasgow, Strathclyde.
A William Adam; C Sir John Maxwell Bt. 1747.
Adam influenced design (if perhaps not actually by him – possibly by Sir John Maxwell himself). Three storeys above a basement, seven by three bays, on the entrance front the central three bays are pedimented.

Poltalloch House, Kilmartin, Argyll.
C William Burn; C Neill Malcolm. 1850.
Sometimes called Callton Mor. A grand Jacobean mansion in spectacular setting with fine views over the estate towards Loch Crinan. Now derelict.

Raith House, Kirkcaldy, Fife.
A James Smith; C Alexander Melville, Lord Raith. 1694.
Significant classical harled seven bay mansion. The central three topped by a pediment with blind oculi.

Rammerscales, Dumfries & Galloway.
A William Craik; C Dr James Mounsey. 1762.
Three storeys above a basement, a tripartite plan and three bays by five. A classical detached block with little ornament.

Ratho Hall, Edinburgh, Midlothian.
A William Burn; C John Bonar. 1824.
Externally the house reveals the functioning of the various interior spaces. The servants' apartments, grouped either side of a communicating corridor, are smaller than the main house. The mansion itself is an almost symmetrical block centred on a mullioned bay window facing the gardens.

Riccarton, Edinburgh, Midlothian.
A William Burn; C Sir William Gibson Craig. 1823.
Jacobean Tudor enlargements to an existing tower house, demolished 1956.

Roseneath Castle, Roseneath, Strathclyde.
A Joseph Bonomi; C 5th Duke of Argyll. 1803.
Neo-classical mansion of the first order. Two storeys on the main entrance facade, above a sunk basement – with the servants' entrance via a tunnel some distance to the rear of the house. Gutted by fire 1947, demolished 1961.

Rowallan House, Kilmaurs, Strathclyde.

A Sir Robert Lorimer; C A. Cameron Corbett MP. 1902.
Scots Baronial mansion, stables, lodges and gardens. Planned about three courts the house was intended to fulfil all the needs associated with its owner's position as an MP.

St Fort, Forgan, Fife.
A William Burn; C Captain Robert Stewart. 1829.
A large Jacobean Tudor manor house. Demolished 1953.

Scone Palace, Scone, Tayside.
A William Atkinson; C 3rd Earl of Mansfield. 1803.
First monastic style mansion house in Scotland, incorporating earlier structures and with a variety of fenestration to enliven the facades. The house makes good use of the naturally sloping site.

Sauchieburn Castle, Stirlingshire.
A Sydney Mitchell & Wilson; C Sir James Maitland Bt. 1890.
A vast Scottish Baronial mansion, somewhat stolid in execution. Demolished.

Seacliffe House, North Berwick, East Lothian.
A David Bryce; C George Sligo. 1841.
Enclosing an earlier house Bryce designed the epitome of his grand Scottish Baronial style – a riot of crow stepped gables, bartizans, and pepper pot turrets.

Skibo Castle, Clashmore, Highland.
A Ross & MacBeth; C Alexander Carnegie. 1900.
Massive remodelling and rebuilding of an existing house to form a large Scottish Baronial castle. Executed in pink sandstone in the most extravagant of styles and used for entertaining Carnegie's political friends.

Stracathro, Tayside.
A Archibald Simpson; C Alexander Cruickshanks. 1828.
Bold classical villa with Corinthian portico.

Now used as a hospital.

Strichen House, Strichen, Banff & Buchan, Grampian.
A John Smith; C Lord Lovat. 1821.
Classical mansion of nine bays by eight, with two storeys. The central three and end bays slightly advanced. The central three have a pediment, and end bays a triumphal arch motif incised. Originally possessing a Doric portico, the facade is now used as the wall to a barn. The house was gutted in 1954.

Symington House, Symington, Strathclyde.
A Andrew Prentice. 1915.
Neo-Georgian mansion of five bays. Three storeys with a neat row of dormer windows accenting the roof. The central three bays are advanced and topped with a balustraded pediment. The end bays are treated as polygonal bow windows on the ground floor with French windows opening onto small balconies above.

Taymouth Castle, Kenmore, Tayside.
A Archibald & James Elliot; C Lord Breadalbane. 1806.
Remodelling of an earlier mansion by William Adam. The Elliots provided a castle in the Neo-Gothic style in a deliberate challenge to Inverary Castle. Subsequently enlarged by William Atkinson (1818) and James Gillespie Graham (1838). As significant an example of Neo-Gothic taste as Inverary.

Tollcross House, Glasgow, Strathclyde.
A David Bryce; C James Dunlop. 1848.
Jacobean Tudor house in the mould of William Burn. Recently restored as private flats. In the care of the NTS.

Tyninghame, Tyninghame, East Lothian.
A William Burn; C 9th Earl of Haddington. 1829.
Scottish Tudor vernacular style, executed in pink sandstone.

Walkinshaw Castle, Paisley, Strathclyde.

A Robert Adam; C D. Macdowall. 1791.
Triangular Adam castle of two storeys above a basement. At the angles of the house were octagonal towers which rose three storeys, linked at the skyline by a balustraded parapet. There were five bays on the entrance front and three bays each on the shorter sides. The house was demolished in 1927.

Wedderburn Castle, Duns, Borders.
A Robert Adam; C Patrick Home. 1768.
Adam castle built about an earlier tower house. Fifteen bay entrance front, octagonal towers at each end, central five bays treated with a castle 'keep' motif.

Yester House, Gifford, East Lothian.
A James Smith & Alexander McGill; C 3rd Marquis of Tweeddale. 1710.
Two main floors above a half sunk rustic the main house was originally nine bays by six. The central three bays are articulated by four Ionic pilasters with a pediment. This entrance front was remodelled by Robert Adam, who provided some interior changes at Yester House as well, in 1789. Either side of the main house are ogee roofed three storey pavilions.

Bibliography

Adam, Robert, *Ruins of the Palace of the Emperor Diocletian at Spalatro in Dalmatia*, London, 1764.

Adam, Robert & James, *The Works in Architecture*, 3 vols., London, 1773–1822, reissued London, 1975.

Adam, William, *Vitruvius Scoticus*, Edinburgh, n.d., reprinted Edinburgh, 1980.

Aslet, Clive, *The Last Country Houses*, London, 1982.

Binney, Marcus; Harris, John, and Winnington, Emma, *Lost Houses of Scotland*, London, 1980.

Beard, Geoffrey, *The Work of Robert Adam*, London, 1978.

Bolton, Arthur, T., *The Architecture of Robert and James Adam*, 2 vols., London, 1922.

Campbell, Colen, *Vitruvius Britannicus*, 3 vols., London, 1715–25, reissued New York, 1967.

Close, Rob, *Ayrshire & Arran, An Illustrated Architectural Guide*, Edinburgh, 1992.

Clough, Monica, *Two Houses*, Aberdeen, 1990.

Colvin, Howard M., *A Biographical Dictionary of British Architects, 1600–1840*, London, 1978.

Cook, Olive, *The English Country House, an Art and a way of Life*, London, 1974.

Cornforth, John, *Country Houses in Britain, Can they survive?*, London, 1972.

Cornforth, John, *The Search for a Style*, London 1988.

Dean, Marcus and Miers, Mary, *Scotland's Endangered Houses*, London, 1990.

Dixon, Roger, and Muthesius, Stefan, *Victorian Architecture*, London 1978.

Dunbar, John G., *The Historic Architecture of Scotland*, London, 1966.

Dunbar, John G., *Sir William Bruce, 1630–1710*, Edinburgh 1970.

Fawcett, Jane (ed.), *Seven Victorian Architects*, London, 1976.

Franklin, Jill, *The Gentleman's Country House and Its Plan*, London, 1981.

Frew, John and Jones, David (eds.), *Aspects of Scottish Classicism*, St Andrews, 1988.

Gifford, John, *Highlands and Islands, Buildings of Scotland*, London, 1992.

Harris, John, *Sir William Chambers, Knight of the Polar Star*, London, 1970.

Jackson-Stops, Gervase (ed.), *The Fashioning and Functioning of the British Country House*, London, 1989.

Macaulay, James, *The Gothic Revival, 1745–1845*, Glasgow & London, 1975.

Macaulay, James, *The Classical Country House in Scotland, 1660–1800*, London, 1987.

MacGibbon, David, and Ross, Thomas, *The Castellated and Domestic Architecture of Scotland*, 5 vols., Edinburgh, 1887–92.

McWilliam, Colin, *Lothian, Buildings of Scotland*, Harmondsworth, 1978.

Methesius, Herman, *The English House*, Berlin, 1904, translated and reprinted London, 1979.

Mordaunt-Crook, J., *The Greek Revival*, London, 1972.

Petzsch, Helmut, *Architecture in Scotland*, London, 1971.

Pevsner, Nikolaus, *Some Architectural Writers of the Nineteenth Century*, Oxford, 1972.

Richardson, Sir Albert, *Robert Mylne, Architect and Engineer, 1783–1811*, London, 1955.

Robinson, John Martin, *The Latest Country Houses*, London 1984.

Rubens, Godfrey, *William Richard Lethaby, His Life and Work, 1857–1931*, London, 1986.

Rykwert, Joseph, and Rkywert, Anne, *The Brothers Adam*, London, 1985.

Savage, Peter, *Lorimer and the Edinburgh Craft Designers*, Edinburgh, 1980.

Serlio, Sebastiano, *The Book of Architecture*, London, 1611, reissued 1970, and reprinted New York, 1980.

Shepherd, Ian A.G., *Grampian, Exploring Scotland's Heritage*, Edinburgh, 1986.

Stamp, Gavin, *Robert Weir Schultz, Architect, and his Work for the Marquess of Bute*, London, 1981.

Tait, A.A., *Treasures in Trust*, Edinburgh, 1981.

Tait, A.A., *Duff House*, Edinburgh, 1985.

Williamson, Elizabeth; Riches, Anne, and Higgs, Malcolm, *Glasgow, Buildings of Scotland*, Town, year.

U'ren, W. Graham (ed.), *Historic Buildings of Clydesdale*, Glasgow, 1987.

Articles:

Colvin, H.M., 'A Scottish origin for English Palladianism?' in *Architectural History*, vol. 17, 1974.

Rowan, Alistair, 'The building of Hopetoun' in *Architectural History*, vol. 27, 1984.

Notes to Chapters

1. Dunbar *The Historic Architecture of Scotland*, p93.
2. Bruce – Annandale 14 September 1694; John Lowery, 'Sir William Bruce and His Circle at Craigiehall 1694–1708 in *Aspects of Scottish Classicism*, p3.
3. Ibid Bruce – Annandale 17 September 1694, p4.
4. Ibid James Macaulay 'The Seventeenth Century Genesis of Hamilton Palace', p19.
5. Dunbar op. cit., p107.
6. Clerk 'The Country Seat', in *The Classical Country House in Scotland 1660–1800*, p70.
7. MacKy *Journey Through Scotland* (1723), in 'The Building of Hopetoun' by Alistair Rowan, Architectural History 1984, Vol. 27, p118.
8. J. Mordaunt-Crook *The Greek Revival*, p17.
9. Adam, Robert & James *The Works in Architecture*, p46.
10. Ibid.
11. Adam, Robert to Sir James Clerk, in *The Classical Country House in Scotland*, p170.
12. Girouard *Life in the English Country House*, p191.
13. Heron in *The Classical Country House in Scotland*, p144.
14. Crook op. cit., p72.
15. Goethe, Ibid, p27.
16. Goethe in Nikolaus Pevsner *Some Architectural Writers of the Nineteenth Century*, p11.
17. Playfair in *Seven Victorian Architects*, p23.
18. Dunbar op. cit., p18.
19. Keer *The Gentleman's House*, p67.
20. Ibid, p68.
21. Lethaby in *The English Country House*, p218.
22. Keer, op. cit., p66.
23. Ibid, p210.
24. William Calder in *The Last Country Houses*, p188.
25. C.V. Butler, *Domestic Service*.
26. Joseph Chamberlain, in *The Last Country House*, p55.
27. John Martin Robinson, *The Latest Country Houses*, p7.

List of Plates

Photographic acknowledgements
The plates in this book are reproduced with the kind permission of the following:
Ordnance Survey © Crown copyright: 28
J Brandon Jones: 71
Neil Jackson: 102
Royal Incorporation of Architects in Scotland Collections: 11, 84
Hamilton District Council Libraries Service: 53
Ayr Carnegie Library: 20
Joe Rock (Photographer): 47
National Monuments Record, held by the Royal Commission on the Ancient and Historical Monuments of Scotland: 1, 4, 6, 7, 8, 9, 10, 17, 19, 21, 22, 23, 24, 25, 26, 27, 29, 30, 34, 35, 38, 43, 44, 46, 48, 49, 51, 52, 58, 62, 63, 65, 68, 69, 70, 74, 75, 87, 96, 97, 98, 101, 103, 104
C Methven-Campbell (RCAHMS): 32
All other plates are copyright of the author.

List of Plans

The plans for this book have been redrawn and adapted by the author from a variety of sources.

Index

173